FEMINISM

In the history of art

FEMINISM

In the history of art

Esther Tauroni Bernabeu

ISBN: 9798651905737

Dedicated to you for being a woman.

To you, Mom, and to the women in my life for, by your example, teaching me the recipe for "I can do more".

Presentation

To speak of feminism is to speak of equality, and making inequalities visible is necessary to eradicate them.

Artistic productions are evidence of different stages of history, mentalities and societies, and therefore are a primary source of incomparable value to visualize the situation of women throughout it.

Through the history of art we can discover and reflect on myths and legends that have created stereotypes of women that survive to this day. We can understand how the reification of female bodies has turned women into sexual objects, the canons of beauty have hidden intellectual gifts, the male gender has hidden the female, spaces have limited existence, roles have annulled lives and violence, besides being justified, has become normal. Through the productions of art history we will understand the imbalances in order to advance towards equality.

Art has had different functions. In some cases its usefulness has been magical-religious, in others it has been aesthetic, ideological, moving, pedagogical, modelling sensibility, ornamental or commercial. With the present issue, the aim is for its function to be, in addition, transformative, to provoke reactions, to make art felt and to advance feminism, that is, to become a socializing agent at the service of an egalitarian society.

Art allows a wide and free democratic development where it is possible to show the differences of gender, culture and socioeconomic level. It is an alternative form of training and education. It is, above all, a powerful means of transmitting values.

In articles that I have written, talks and debates that I have organised or workshops that I have coordinated, I have seen, first hand, how a work of art attracts and is, as well as a communication tool, a starting point for spaces of expression that activate inclusion, personal and social transformation.

Art has a universal language that overcomes language and generational barriers, it transmits experiences where individual and common experiences can be recognised, it favours and stimulates social change. It is, in short, a fabulous instrument for generating environments of expression, encounter, participation and personal development. Spaces that allow us to transcend difficulties and, for the specific case of this specimen, to evidence the inequality that women experience and to advance, jointly, towards equality.

Expression is a dimension and a fundamental right of people, and artistic expression is a privileged way for us, especially those who face situations of exclusion or vulnerability, to develop, claim and exercise their rights.

Some known, and others perhaps not, works from the Renaissance, Baroque, avant-garde and contemporary movements; from different schools, artists, countries or institutions that keep them, will bring us closer in this book to dialogue with art and to find in their works reasons to talk about feminism.

I therefore invite women and men who are aware of social imbalances and who firmly believe in gender equality to look at the works I propose at the beginning of each chapter, to observe them, to feel them and to think about them. Then read them critically, question the opinions expressed, and be enriched by those that are similar. And, in the end, to transform, to grow, to increase the empathy towards the women, to evidence and to recognize personal, familiar or foreign situations. To understand that art is an unquestionable tool in education for equality.

I hope that, after reading this issue, being in front of a work of art is an opportunity not only for delight but also to understand that it is an opportunity for reflection, dialogue and debate about the content that each work has.

Index

Foreword

Gender-based violence is a social scourge that affects everyone. Women because they are the direct victims; men because they are partners, fathers, sons, brothers and have healthy ties to women.

Feminism and education in equality is the key to eradicating violence. And it is not a matter of educating those who are in school, but of doing so to the entire population by preventing, raising awareness and sensitizing. The productions of art history, as a reflection of society, are a magnificent pedagogical tool to make inequalities visible, move consciences and open necessary debates.

The entry into force of the Comprehensive Law against Gender Violence (LO 1/2004) created a climate of hope in order to tackle the reality of women victims of gender violence. However, neither this law nor the State Pact against Gender Violence has been a panacea to tackle it, but rather it has continued to increase. Currently, the rates of gender violence are increasingly high among the young.

In Spain, 1.4 million women have been victims of sexual violence. Every 8 hours a woman is raped in our country. So far this year, the number of women murdered by their partners or ex-partners does not stop growing. Violence against women, and their children - a new form of aggression against women - needs to be addressed in all its severity.

Murder and rape are the tip of the iceberg. Invisibility, control, exclusivity, isolation, annulment and emotional blackmail are subtle and invisible forms of this violence. Contempt, humiliation and threats are also invisible. Shouting, insults, physical aggression and abuse are not only evident, but are also the preludes to dramatic endings. These and other manifestations are nourished by the patriarchal system.

In too many sectors these social behaviors are normalized. Society seems resigned to the existence of this very serious problem that is usually understood as a domestic matter that only affects the parties involved when it is really of a social and community nature.

Today's society and future generations need tools to exercise criticism and discern the macho content that we breathe daily at all levels, from those that are part of everyday life to those that reach us from the media, advertising and the Internet.

Traditionally, artistic productions have been studied from their formal description, losing the opportunity to contribute to training and socialization. It is time to understand art as a transmitter of culture, of feelings, of experiences, of dialogue. Art reveals stories, intentionality, meanings, ideas, some intrinsic and others that we can create according to the conception of our world. Fleeing from the utilitarianism and objectivism of art history, analysing other issues different from forms and their use or the mastery of technique, we will find in art history the history of the expression of ideas, feelings, culture and human folklore. And as such it must be understood, studied and transmitted to new generations who will thus see their lives enriched from many more fronts than the purely formal.

Above and beyond individualities, geographical or economic origins, the history of art must be understood as the history of creativity, opening up new ways of understanding the universe and expressing it. Artistic productions reveal the impartiality with which women have been represented, the male ghost that created them, the stereotypes and archetypes in female figuration, their creations, the false myths, legends and stories that the works hide. In short, to offer less individualistic, ethnocentric and androcentric visions, making women and men participants in a story in process, susceptible of internal criticism, which shows its transforming usefulness in society.

The images must be subjected to a decoding process that allows not only their reading but also their full enjoyment. To deprive the human being of the capacity to understand and enjoy the image, to be moved by it, is to deprive him/her of part of his/her potential.

With a gender perspective, I propose to bring art closer to citizens and women's reality closer to art with the aim of discovering in the former a magnificent tool that makes visible the history that the female world has lived through and, in the latter, the scourge of male violence.

To observe the works proposed in each chapter, to think, to feel, to read the subjective opinions that are expressed, to invite to dialogue, to contrast ideas and to expose different points of view are the intentions of this author in the present issue. Whether one agrees or not, the important thing is not to leave the reader indifferent. Creating debate is the ultimate goal.

Sensitizing, preventing and raising awareness about existing inequalities between different genders is the issue. Advocating for equality, the solution.

Myths, legends, stories, works of male authorship, female images and women's stories, are the background to the analysis of works of art that invite to talk about social imbalances, feelings and realities in a feminist key, revealing irrationalities of the present moment.

FROM BEING AN ECHO TO BEING A SHOUT: MARCH 8

John William Waterhouse "Echo and Narcissus". Oil on canvas. 236x107 cm. 1908. Walker Art Gallery, UK.

Centuries of patriarchal culture, of submission, imbalance and inequality have kept women silenced and only allowed a repetitive and reiterative discourse invented by androcentrism, to extol and empower male qualities and make female needs invisible. It is nauseating that when women have demanded equality and claimed to have a presence in public spaces, some sectors, intimidated by this, have said that we shout, shout, scandalize, "we are with the rule" or we are provocative, a misogynist nonsense that reveals the fear of losing the servitude that we have been for them.

Patriarchy requires power, submission, subjugation, slavery and silence on the part of those who believed they were concubines of their harem, in the best of cases they have allowed us to be their echoes, and it is interesting to go deeper into the origin of the concepts.

Many artists, among them the English pre-Raphaelite John Waterhouse, were inspired by the legend of Echo to conceive one of his works, in this case an oil on canvas today in the Walker Art Gallery executed in 1903. The painting is entitled "Echo and Narcissus", a legend told in "The Metamorphoses of Ovid", and exemplifies the vital differences we have experienced due to the genre: while in a bucolic forest Narcissus, indifferent to the presence of Echo, falls in love with his own image, she, with an absolutely objectified body, is silent, observes and waits.

Like all the women who appear in the paintings, unless they are witches, madwomen, old ladies or whores, Echo is immensely beautiful, sweet, placid, serene and of course shows her breast to the voyeuristic spectator. Narcissus bronze, muscular and covered does not need to show any attribute to be beautiful.

In mythology Echo was a nymph who stood out from the rest for her words, her intonation, her expression, which she gave to the ears that heard her, her phrases were assimilated into songs, her prayers into poems, her virtue was in her speech. Zeus, the god of the gods, was enraptured by her, which bothered his wife Hera. So, jealously, he punished Echo by suppressing her voice, her power to express herself, and condemned her to repeat the last word spoken by the person with whom she was in conversation. Hera's jealousy, provoked by her husband's incessant infidelities, denied Echo her precious gift, her capacity to express herself, to relate and to have initiatives for the rest of her life. They subdued her and set her apart in a hidden field.

In absolute solitude, and walking on the hillside, Echo saw Narcissus, a shepherd son of the nymph Liriope and the river god Cepheus, with whom she fell in love as many women had done and whom she had rejected.

Echo followed him without him noticing. When he decided to come closer the words refused to come out of his mouth and he hid behind a dry tree. In the meantime Narcissus was talking to the flowers in the forest:

Beautiful flower, smelly flower...

- Rosa," repeated Echo.

Narcissus heard Echo's voice and shouted: - Is there anyone here?

- Here, here," answered the nymph.

Narcissus heard Echo and answered: "Who is hiding near that dry tree?

And the beautiful nymph came out of the trees with open arms saying: - Echo, Echo.

Nemesis, goddess of vengeance, heard his plea. In a quiet valley there was a pond, of clear water, which had never been muddy, neither by the mire nor by the snouts of the cattle. Narcissus arrived at this lake and when he lay down on the grass to drink, Cupid stuck his arrow of love in his back... the first thing Narcissus saw was his own image reflected in the clear waters and he believed that the beautiful face he was contemplating was that of a real being, alien to himself. He fell in love with those eyes that shone like stars, with those dull cheeks, with that slender neck, with those black hairs. He had fallen in love with himself and no longer cared about anything but his image. He stayed a long time contemplating himself in the pond and, little by little, he took in the fresh colours of those apples, red on one side, white and golden on the other, slowly transforming himself into a very beautiful flower that at the edge of the waters continued to be contemplated in the mirror of the lake. At the same moment that Narcissus was transformed into a flower, Echo crumbled into the grass, dead with love.

Echo's body could never be found, but through the mountains and valleys, in all parts of the world, it still responds to the last syllables of human voices. Those last syllables are the ones that the patriarchy has forced us to repeat to women as if we were an acoustic phenomenon of their own voices.

Centuries of silence, of obedience, of legends, myths and traditions that have condemned women to seclude themselves in a remote corner of the private sphere seem to have begun to be clarified with the feminist waves that have given back to the female gender its voice and that, at the top of its voice, claims for equality. The concept of crying is a curious one, given that the patriarchy itself associates it with hysteria, lack of control, emotionalism and sentimentalism, which also stigmatises women, when in fact the cry, which etymologically comes from the Latin quiritare, refers to calling for help and, precisely the quirites were the citizens, civilians or Roman peasants who opposed the army and soldiers in ancient Rome.

Quirino, god of war, protected them. Thus, more than 20 centuries later, we find forms of expression typical of the oppressed classes in the face of the dominant classes, of society in the face of power. And we do it in the Quirinale, ancient hill of Rome and, metaphorically, today public space where to demand the equality of opportunities between men and women.

On March 8, 1857, in New York, hundreds of women from a textile factory demonstrated in the streets of the city claiming that their wages were less than half of what men were paid for the same task. The day ended with 120 women killed in the march and the founding, by the survivors, of the first women's union.

In 1975, the UN made March 8 official as International Women's Day and, since then, with more force in recent years, for us this date is a reference in the visibility of the political, economic and social vulnerability that we live, the inequalities and injustices that we endure in a patriarchal and capitalist system in which, despite whoever it may be, women advance accompanied by parents, children, couples and men in solidarity, aware and conscious of the need for equality that we need in this necessary and beneficial struggle for one and all.

On March 8, women need to stop being echoes and demand that the way out of this world of care and attention to which we have been relegated and which, in addition to not being paid or recognized, is the basis of good functioning and social balance.

GENIUS, GENIUS AND GENIUS: DORA MAAR.

Dora Maar "Self-Photography". 1935.

It is well known that too many sectors make fun of and despise us when we try to democratize our language, make it inclusive, and divide it up in order to feminize it and integrate ourselves. From "miembro to miembra", as from "genio" to "genia", there is the same step, so I will talk about genius, which, besides being feminine, is an ideal qualifier to talk about the artistic production of Dora Maar, who had the misfortune of being part of Pablo

33

Picasso's album of cards that stated that "The woman genius does not exist; when she exists she is a man".

Since the time of ancient Rome, the word "Genius" was a masculine noun referring to a deity that was conceptualized as the divine incarnation of the capacity to create that resided in the mind of man. Genius became a kind of guardian spirit, spreading the belief that each man who was the head of the family had his own "Genius", and was also the protector of the other members of the family group. Later, the idea spread that each place or organization had its own genius (genius loci or genius populi).

From the concept "genius" the concept of artist was constructed and applied to the masculine, without accepting until today the feminine equivalent and, of course not qualifying in the artistic or scientific field to women with such designation which also leads us to meditate on the idea of why great women artists have remained anonymous. The fact is that, since ancient times, people have believed in the non-existence of female geniuses, arguing the supposed cultural and intellectual inferiority of women, and as history has advanced, despite the fact that the intelligence of men and women has been shown to be equal, the productions of women have had less repercussion and recognition, since socially they did not form part of public space.

We find ourselves, then, with the concession of female merits such as that of copyist, amateur, follower, imitator, disciple of a genius, but never catalogued as such.

Therefore, without falling into the debate on genius or genius, and without using the masculine to refer to women in my speech, I opt for the concept of "genius" to refer to women artists who have stood out for their innovation, creativity, determination and authenticity.

Dora Maar is one example among thousands. She was a French surrealist artist, painter, sculptor and photographer whose professional career was cut short when she met Pablo Ruiz Picasso who, attracted and bewitched by a talent superior to his, spent the years he spent with her belittling her work, nullifying it and making her part of his entourage. When Dora entered Picasso's life, she entered the circle of violence, in an escalation that ended when he got her, after 10 years of mistreatment, to affirm that "After Picasso, only God". Having accepted this, the Malaga-born man hated her and abandoned her.

Dora Maar was one of the seven women-couples visible in Picasso's life. They met in 1936, she was 29, he was 55, married to Olga Koklova and expecting a daughter from Marie-Thérèse Walter, whom he named Maya. The relationship ended when in 1947 Picasso met François Gillot, who was 21 and whom he impregnated first with Claude and then with Paloma.

Her original name was Henriette Theodora Markovitch. She was born in Tours, France, on November 22, 1907 and died in Paris in 1997. Her father was an architect, and her mother a violinist gave Dora a wealthy and cultivated life. She spoke French, Croatian and Spanish, as she lived her adolescence in Argentina. Once in

France, she began her studies at the Academie Lothe, and later entered L'École de Photographie de la Ville de Paris, and after some incursions into the world of painting, it was here that she managed to stand out.

His first steps in the world of photography were taken in Harry Meerson's studio, later he began to work with, also a photographer, Pierre Keffer with whom he collaborated in fashion magazines such as "Madame Figaro" and in campaigns for cosmetics whose protagonist was Assia (muse par excellence of the surrealist movement). During these years, his favourite subjects were photographs of female faces and nudes, very daring for those years, as well as dreamy, dreamy landscapes, captivating because of their ambiguous readings. The faces, superimposed, were also an innovation in this art. In his work he sought to break with convention by freely associating images, seeking hidden forms and creating different realities that were suggestive for the spectator. To a certain extent they were dark, mystical, enigmatic works that revealed his intelligent, melancholic and complex character.

From the Dadaist Man Ray he learned the technique of blurring and experimented with photomontage, fotocollage and overprinting; from Giorgio de Chirico he nourished himself to idealize his images and architectures in the irrational metaphysics of dreams, wrapping his work in an enigmatic halo, "Silence", "Cavaliers" and "Rue d'Astorg" are examples of this.

As well as being an artist, Dora Maar was an activist, a vindicator and extraordinarily sensitive to the political and social events that were taking place in the mid-1930s. Thus, after coming into contact in 1934 with the French writer and anthropologist George Bataille, she decided to travel to Spain on the eve of the war and, in Barcelona, she began a series of photographs where she captured the reality of misery, poverty, desperation and marginalisation through beggars, children and women who wandered the working class neighbourhoods of Barcelona. Later, in Paris and London, she became a tenacious leftist activist who denounced her indignation with her photographs.

In 1936 she met Picasso and became the most valuable witness of the evolution of the "Guernica", photographing every cog in the creative process, the painter at different times, the work started and finished. That same year he also produced one of his most famous works "The Portrait of Ubú", the main character of Alfred Jarry's play "Ubú Rey" and whose image became a photographic icon of surrealism.

Dora's relationship with Picasso was opposed by her father and mother from the beginning, both because of the age difference and because of the Malaga man's unbalanced and womanly reputation. However, she, in love, ignored his views and turned to the painter and isolated herself. Picasso despised her art, for him photography had no value and neither did the meaning she gave to it, he humiliated her and made fun of her while trying to train her with the brushes. At the same time, like other women, Picasso made Dora his model and muse, whom he always painted sad and crying.

Witnesses and friends claimed that both psychologically and physically the painter mistreated the photographer, the genius the genius. Faced with the humiliations, Dora became unbalanced and, due to her irrational behaviour, Jacques Lacan psychoanalysed her and recommended her admission to the Sainte-Anne hospital where she was subjected to electroshock. Paul Éluard, Dora's friend and Dadaist poet, accused Picasso of making her suffer too much. By then the 61-year-old from Malaga had already met François Gillot, 21, with whom he had a relationship.

Sick and unable to choose an artistic path that would alleviate her pain, from 1945 until her death in 1997 Dora Maar's artistic career, which had been as prolific as it was remarkable, fell into absolute decline, marking her life, from then on, with recollection and refuge in the religion locked up in her Paris studio. In her will she left her assets (including 130 Picassos and most of her photographs) to a monk.

Dora Maar's name was eclipsed in the painter's shadow and she hid the best photographer of the Surrealist movement as well as one of the pioneers of documentary photojournalism.

Psychological abuse leads to fear, anxiety, depression, anger, stress, isolation, dependence and generates devastating wounds that haunt the victims for many years, even throughout their lives, stealing life projects and preventing them from enjoying a full existence. Dora Maar was a victim of this, but she must not also be a victim of the forgetfulness of her genius, since despite living in the shadow of Picasso, she surpassed him in talent.

THE VASES OF THE PATRIARCHY: THE PORTRAIT OF AMALIA DE LLANO BY FEDERICO DE MADRAZO.

Federico de Madrazo and Kunt "Portrait of the Countess of Vilches". Oil on canvas. 126 x 89 cm. 1853. Prado Museum.

Throughout history, women have made very important contributions to the world of mathematics, physics, biology, literature and art, and we have done so under particularly difficult conditions. The patriarchy has been in charge of undervaluing and even making invisible our discoveries and findings and the images of women showing them devoid of any intellectual dowry, turning us into decorative objects like vases, candlesticks, paintings or tapestries to make the corners of the home more pleasant.

Female portraiture shows that women, regardless of whether they are scientists, writers, painters or engaged in any other field of knowledge, are portrayed as women without iconographic elements that provide the viewer with information about their knowledge, which is not the case in male portraits. Books, awards, instruments, staffs and weapons accompany male characters in the story who tell us about their heroics or exploits, while women pose as orphans of elements that distinguish them.

Aristotelian philosophy, which is the main reference in Western thought, was a pernicious idea that has survived until the present day, considering women to be inferior both physically, psychologically and morally, even "mere empty vessels of the recipient of creative semen". In his work, "History of the Animals", Aristotle establishes the differences between the sexes and affirms that Nature has given them different mental characteristics. For the philosopher, women have a gentler disposition, more compassionate, more inclined to cry, more impulsive, more jealous, more distrustful, more cowardly, more false, more inclined to murmur and to anger; they possess less shame and dignity, are less active and require less food, but are more careful with their offspring and have greater memory. Incredible as they may seem to us, these labels have survived for nearly 25 centuries resulting in images that are kind, sweet, even flirtatious, anything but intellectual.

One of the great masters of Spanish female portraiture is Federico de Madrazo, who is also a magnificent representative of Romanticism and for whom writers of the stature of Gertrudis Gómez de Avellaneda and Carolina Coronado posed. Her work "The Countess of Vilches", which is Amalia de Llano y Dotres, is one of the pictorial peaks of the 19th century and one of the most emblematic of the Prado Museum. Amalia was a writer, political activist, actress and director of plays and literary gatherings. Through her portrait we could not imagine what she was.

Amalia de Llano was born in Barcelona on 29 April 1822. Her father, Ramon de Llano Chávarri, and her mother, Pilar Dotres Gibert, belonged to the wealthy Catalan bourgeoisie. When her father died, her mother married the IX Marquis of Almonacid, Francisco Falcó y Varcárcel, which allowed them to enter aristocratic circles. At the age of 17, in October 1839, she married Gonzalo de Vilches y Parga, 14 years older than her, and with whom she had a son and a daughter, Gonzalo and Pilar. In 1848, Queen Isabel II ennobled Amalia's husband by naming him Count, so she became Countess.

Amalia made her reproduction and care tasks compatible with reading and writing, managing to publish two novels "Ledia" and "Berta", as well as participating in and organizing plays, musicals and literary meetings attended by intellectuals and artists of the time, one of them being Federico de Madrazo who portrayed her when she was 32 years old, in 1853. Her death, when she was only 52 years old, was very felt in Madrid and several articles were published in the press of the time, recognizing her as an active figure in the cultural life of the nineteenth century capital. She was buried in the family pantheon in the cemetery of San Isidro.

Amalia's portrait, and oil on canvas measuring 126 x 89 cm, is full of charm, refinement and refinement, with a very "chic" and French air and a sensual posture that enhances the whiteness of the flesh with the dark background and the lively dress. Her seductive smile, her sweet gaze and the delicacy with which she holds the fan, give the work the label of pride, insofar as each brushstroke masks who this woman was.

Being a magnificent portrait because of its style, treatment, composition and colour, the truth is that either by the artist's choice or by the protagonist's decision, Amalia, in spite of having broken with the stereotypes of her time, prolongs them in the work. A pen to write with or a book in her hands could have replaced the range of pens she carries, but perhaps neither one nor the other was designed to discover the talents of women, it being preferable to continue showing them as angels of her home or magnificent vases.

In the mid-19th century the French philosopher Charles Pierre Baudelaire stated that "*In every woman of letters there is a failed man*" and Nietzsche that "*When a woman has learned inclinations, there is usually something wrong with her sexuality*". In the middle of the 20th century Freud declared that "*Girls suffer all their lives the trauma of penis envy after discovering that they are anatomically incomplete*"; Carl G. Jung that "*By following a masculine vocation, studying and working like a man, a woman does something that does not correspond entirely to her feminine nature, but is harmful*" and Ortega y Gasset that "*The strength of a woman is not to know but to feel. To know things is to have*

*concepts and definitions, and this is the
work of the man"*.

A whole literature and misogynist
philosophical thought is condensed in this
wonderful portrait that hides
Schopenhauer's message, who emphasized
that *"Only the aspect of woman reveals that
she is not destined for the great works of
the intelligence nor for the great material
works"*. Thus, the aspect of women
continues until today to enhance their
femininity which, in too many cases, is
equivalent to hiding their intellectuality.

RESPONSIBLE PARENTING IN THE WORK OF MARGARITA SIKORSKAIA.

Margarita Sikorskaia "Listening". 2007

The battle to extend paternity leave is another of the feminist struggles that seems to matter little to men, when it comes to a benefit for their quality of life and enjoyment of daughters and family life. According to data from the Spanish Ministry of Labour, the number of paternity benefits managed by the Social Security in 2018 amounted to 255,531, 3.4% less than in 2017, at a cost of over 448 million euros. In other words, fewer and fewer parents are taking advantage of this right.

Paternity leave was approved in 2007 through Organic Law 3/2007, of 22 March, on Effective Equality between Men and Women, and was implemented as a measure to support the reconciliation of personal, family and working life. It lasted 13 days, which could be extended in the case of multiple births by 2 more days for each child from the second, and was also extended for cases of adoption or foster care. In 2015 it was extended to 20 days, although it did not become effective until January 2016. A year later, in 2017, it was set at 4 weeks; from 1 April 2019, to 8 weeks and, currently, from 1 January 2020, to 12 weeks. However, and despite institutional efforts, parenthood is still not understood as the obligation to exercise it in co-responsibility. Culturally, it is exercised from the birth of the child, when it should occur from the beginning of the gestation.

The enjoyment of life, happiness, love and peace produced by motherhood and fatherhood, especially when it is shared, is magnified in the work of Margarita Sikorskaia, a Russian painter currently living in the United States, whose work "Listening" is a good example of this.

Margarita was born in 1968 in St. Petersburg and studied at the Department of Arts and Graphics of the Hertzen Pedagogical University, where she was naturally influenced by the works of masters and artists of socialist realism. The current critics see in her work influences of Fernando Botero's style (because of the volumetry of her figures), but they affirm it ignoring her cradle and formation.

Between the 1930s and 1950s in the Soviet Union a totalitarian regime was established that used art as propaganda, with the purpose of educating and ideologizing the masses in the spirit of socialism. The aim was to give an image of a unitary, just, egalitarian and prosperous state in which, thanks to the triumph of socialism, the citizenry was happy and full of enthusiasm. Of course, the artists echoed this in their works. Alexander Gerasimov, Vasily Efanov, Alexander Deineka and Alexander Samojválov enjoyed success and prestige. Realistic art was promoted, with solemn and majestic figures reflecting parades, visits, images of leaders, wise men, but friends of the people. Scenes of the industrial boom, of the benefits of collectivity, of peasant glories, of the importance of each individual, regardless of sex, in the construction of a revolutionary country. Strong spirits with visible contours were the protagonists of the plastic arts.

Taken to her family's land, Margarita Sikorskaia transferred this ideology to her work, which, early on, triumphed in the United States, where she moved to live when she was 22 years old, in 1990, and where she currently lives, works and triumphs as an artist. In 2000 she was selected to participate in the Minnesota Biennial and since then she has had collective and individual exhibitions in

New Orleans, Minneapolis and Moorhead, among others.

Margarita's work smells of love, the curved bodies, embraced, giving affection, mimes, tenderness, with intense colors under a luminous sky inspire instinct and shelter. Couples, maternity wards, everyday domestic scenes, empowered women breastfeeding and protecting their children, rough men showing their sensitivity and tenderness are the protagonists of her work. Despite the grandiloquence, these are moving images that radiate happiness and passion for life.

In "Listening", we discover the man we have wanted to have close to us at the moment of pregnancy, when our bodies change and our emotions come to the surface, when stretch marks appear, legs swell, when our baby kicks and needs warm hands to calm him down. In Sikorskaia's work, man and woman are equal, complementary, co-responsible and lovers. There is no erotic, sexual or discriminatory charge, only affection and emotion that please those who enjoy the scene.

In the patriarchal culture we live in, the image may seem utopian, but it is not unreal or unattainable. It should not be considered a myth or a dream but the pending subject of men and fathers for having the opportunity to express their feelings and emotions, so far and in view of the data, unrealizable.

With serenity, maturity, harmony and union, the couple in this work embrace the future in the equality needed by the son or daughter to come. A future that will avoid violence and guarantee freedom.

VANESSA BELL AND VIRGINIA WOOLF: THE EXTRAORDINARY STEPHEN SISTERS.

Vanessa Bell "self-portrait." Óleo sobre lienzo. 45x37 cm. 1958.

Better known as Vanessa Bell and Virginia Woolf, both were sisters and daughters of Leslie Stephen and Julia Prinsep but, because of the Anglo-Saxon custom of adopting the husband's surname upon marriage, the story obscures the link between the brilliant painter that was Vanessa and the illustrious writer that was Virginia. Another burden of male chauvinism.

Leslie and Julia were married when they were both widowed, so he brought a daughter into the marriage (Laura) and she brought three children (George, Stella and Gerald). He was a novelist, historian, biographer and mountaineer; she was a famous beauty and a model for the pre-Raphaelite people. The couple, in their relationship, had two daughters and two sons: Vanessa, Thoby, Virginia and Adrian. Laura, Leslie's daughter, was suffering from serious mental problems and lived with the family until she had to be admitted to a psychiatric hospital in 1891. She was 21 years old, Vanessa 12 years old and Virginia 9 years old. Her half-sister's illness marked them both forever.

In 1879 Vanessa was born; in 1882, Virginia, both at 22 Hyde Park Gate, in Kensington, London, and raised by her father and mother in a literary environment full of good relations. They did not go to school but received private lessons at home. The family's holiday periods were spent in Cornwall, its beaches, its lighthouse, its waters and its light influenced the life and work of the sisters. Vanessa painted their landscapes, Virginia was inspired by those lands. From their house "Thailand House" they saw the lighthouse of Godrevy that, in Vanessa, served as a frame for many impressionist landscapes in which she played with light and color and in Virginia to write "The Lighthouse". The sisters had a close and enriching relationship and, the circumstances of suffering both sexual abuses by their brothers, the sudden death of their mother when the oldest was 16, and the youngest at 13, her half sister Stella two years later, and her father, being 26 and 23 years old respectively, brought them closer together making Vanessa the caretaker and responsible for the home.

The limited circumstances they lived through made them peculiar, strong women, marked by a stormy childhood that in the future provoked bipolar behavior in Virginia and Vanessa into a sexually and sentimentally free woman, without commitments, predecessor of the queer movement. Virginia in her famous "Mrs. Donoway", described her sister with a golden jug full of water, from which, however, never a drop was spilled. It was and always has been her older sister, the one who pampered and cared for her and, although eclipsed by her fame, her most fervent admirer.

In 1905, after the death of their father, both sisters sold the house where they lived in Hyde Park and bought one at 46 Gordon Square in Bloomsburry, turning it into a centre for meetings and gatherings where the London intelligentsia went. In addition to them, the meetings were attended by Clive Bell (art critic), E. M. Forster (fiction writer), Roger Fry (critic and painter), Duncan Grant (painter), John Maynard Keynes (economist), Desmond MacCarthy (literary critic). Lytton Strachey (biographer) and Leonard Woolf (essayist and writer), among others. The so-called "Bloomsbury Circle" was thus a heterogeneous group that shared a contempt for religion, Victorian morality and realism; their liberal and humanist ideology philosophically defended the importance of personal relations and private life; socially, they rejected bourgeois habits and the search for personal pleasure; politically, they held leftist and feminist positions; artistically, they defended the significant form, post-impressionism.

A consequence of that thought was the well-known joke known as "The Dreadnought's Deception", which consisted in the fact that in February 1910 several members of the Circle, including Virginia, disguised, made up and dressed up as an Abyssinian royal family who demanded to be received with all the necessary pomp by the British royal navy. The deception, besides causing effect, caught the attention of the press of the time and highlighted the existence of a circle of intellectuals created by two sisters, Vanessa and Virginia, the Stephen sisters.

In 1907, Vanessa married art critic Clive Bell; in 1912, Virginia married writer Leonard Woolf. In none of the relationships there was exclusivity, they were open couples and also bisexual.

Professionally, Vanessa was one of the introducers of impressionism in England and one of the greatest exponents in all of Europe. She was one of the most influential portraitists of the 20th century, as well as one of the first experimenters in photography and designer of the original covers of her sister Virginia's books. She died in 1961 as a result of a heart attack and has been forgotten and eclipsed for years by the glow of her sister Virginia. However, her work began to be valued and rediscovered by organizing a retrospective of her work in 2017 at the Dulwich Picture Gallery in London.

Virginia had committed suicide 20 years earlier, victim of continuous depressions and nervous breakdowns. Her hypersensitivity has given the narrative and philosophy works summits of feminist thought "Orlando: a biography" (1928), "The waves" (1931) "The haunted house" or "A room of their own" (1927) expose with simplicity the difficult existence of women. "Una habitación propia" is a true banner of the feminist movement, since it relates the difficulties of women to be able to dedicate themselves to the world of writing in a world dominated by men. Among its famous phrases are:

"There is no barrier, lock or bolt you can impose o n the freedom of my mind."

"Life is a dream; waking up is what kills us"

"As a woman I have no country, as a woman I want no country. As a woman, my homeland is the world."

"Loving separates us from others"

"And once again she felt alone in the presence of her eternal antagonist: life.

"To grow up is to lose some illusions and start having others."

"Through suffering, knowledge is attained"

"Why are women... much more interesting to men than men are to women?"

"It's much harder to kill a ghost than a reality."

"For most of history, 'Anonymous' was a woman."

Virginia Woolf's work, without a doubt, is a reference for all of us; Vanessa Bell's is a pictorial production that has been unjustly made invisible; both of them, in addition to a link, have created an intellectual, renovating and regenerating group such as the Bloomsbury Circle. Two exceptional women, sisters, lovers, admired artists and portentous in the personal and intellectual sense.

LENA KRASNER, THE WOMAN ECLIPSED BY JACKSON POLLOCK.

Lena Krasner "Noon". Oil on canvas. 1947

In the acidic irony that characterized them in 1989, the Guerrilla Girls claimed that women artists had many advantages over men. First, they could afford to work without the pressure of success; second, they had the opportunity to choose between their career and their motherhood; third, they could have the satisfaction of seeing their ideas reflected in the work of others; fourth, they could be confident that whatever they did would be catalogued as women's art; fifth and finally, they could be certain that the art produced by women would be included in versions that would be revised until they disappeared from art history. This is, and continues to be, a reality that those of us in the artistic field who seek to neutralize gender and sex in order to speak of artists must dismantle, and in this rescue and revision we must undoubtedly place the work of Lena Krasner, perhaps the greatest and best representative of abstract expressionism, but in the shadow of her husband Jackson Pollock, whom she cared for and calmed in her self-destruction and alcoholism by renouncing the visibility of her own work.

In a conference in 1973, in an Art forum, the painter lamented this:

"It is a pity that women's liberation did not occur 30 years earlier in my life. I could not run away and do my work as a woman artist in a world as sexist as the art world, I

could not continue with my painting and remain in the role I was in as Mrs. Pollock".

Lena's frustration would have been greater had she known that 30 years later a painting by her husband would be paid $140 million, the highest price ever paid for a painting, while she was still known as Mrs. Pollock regardless of her work.

Lena Krasner was the sixth child of a Jewish couple from Russia who settled in the United States. She was the only descendant born on the American continent, in 1908, in Brooklyn, New York. Lena always wanted to be an artist and, despite the fact that her family did not support her much, she studied at the school of Hans Hofmann who described her work as follows: "It is a work so good that nobody would know that it was made by a woman". The words of her teacher prompted her to change her first name from "Lena" to the ambiguous "Lee," with which she became known in the artistic arena, establishing herself as one of the earliest and most innovative figures of abstract expressionism, and in 1940 she began to exhibit her work alongside other painters, thus promoting the movement. In that professional circle and in those years she met, in Mexico, Jackson Pollock with whom she married in 1945.

Pollock, of Irish descent, came from a family of farmers. He was born in 1912 in Cody, Wyoming. Because of the work of his father, who was a surveyor, he lived in different states around the country. Artistically inclined, he enrolled in the Los Angeles Manual Arts High School in the 1930s from which he was expelled, so he continued to accompany his father at work and dedicated himself to exploring the culture of the native peoples of the United States until he moved to New York. There he studied with his brother and tried to deal with his alcoholism problem by undergoing Jungian psychotherapy between 1938 and 1941 (he was only 26 years old) with Dr. Joseph L. Henderson who encouraged him to draw and got him hooked on painting. The Jungian concepts and archetypes were expressed in his paintings, and recently some historians have pointed to the painter's suffering from bipolar disorder.

When they got married, Lena was four years older than Jackson and, thanks to a loan, they were able to buy a house with a wooden barn at 830 Springs Fireplace Street, outside New York. Pollock turned the barn into his studio, a large open space where he perfected his technique of painting large "splashes" with which he succeeded and felt fully identified. Lena, in a small room inside the house, piled up canvases, brushes, shaves and dyes that only allowed her to execute Little Images. The "Own Room" that Virginia Woolf had described a few years earlier reduced Lena's possibilities, while the large barn allowed her husband to produce large-scale works. Two spaces, two worlds, one limited for her, one infinite for him.

The spaciousness of the space allowed Pollock to dispense with traditional materials such as the easel and brushes, being able to leave large canvases on the floor or hang them on the walls where he could experiment with all the strength of his body. He walked around his works, went inside, danced, built and destroyed with gardening shovels, knives, diluted paint, sand, broken glass or any material he could find. He lost consciousness inside his paintings and felt that when he lost contact with them the result was a disaster. Pollock would uncontrollably pour his strength against the canvas by throwing, pouring, dripping or splashing materials. Lena in her reduced space, having to take care of her alcoholic husband, bear his self-destructive ups and downs, manage his work and promote and market his art, saw how her production stopped, limiting herself to making small format works and some collages.

Through contacts and friends, Krasner tried to promote her husband's work, finding in art critic Greenberg a strong support by writing favorable articles for the artist. In her idea to stop giving titles to his works and to devote herself to numbering them, she also found support from her husband who said: *"He used to give his paintings conventional names... but now he just numbered them. The numbers are neutral. They make people see the painting for what it is, pure painting"*, Pollock's work quickly escalated. In 1949,

Life magazine devoted a four-page article to him asking, *"Is he the greatest living painter in America?* "He was only 37 years old and had become a genius. Pollock had received many commissions from collectors and, unable to cope with them, he increasingly turned to alcohol and strained his relationship with his wife to the extreme, falling into the abyss of non-productivity.

Pollock, also known as a womanizer, in early 1956 met Ruth Kligman, a voluptuous 26-year-old former model who became his lover. Lena Krasner, upon learning of the relationship, left on a trip to Europe and Ruth settled in the couple's home, encouraging her lover to paint but he did not want to. In August of the same year, driving under the influence of alcohol and carrying Ruth and another friend in her car, Pollock died in an accident and Ruth, who survived, was nicknamed by the poet Frank O'Hara as "the girl in the car of death". According to her, before the accident she produced her last work, "Red, Black & Silver," whose authorship is still in doubt.

Lena Krasner, despite her husband's bad reputation, took care of her business and kept her work alive despite the changing trends in art. She labeled her relationship with Kligman as "My Five Fucks with Jackson Pollock, because that's it" and after burying her husband, she released her anger, took her work material out of the small room, placed it in the barn next to her talent and began to make large format series. She was 48 years old when she regained the reins of her life.

Lena had been trained in post-impressionism and cubism with which she experimented until abstract impressionism, however, personal circumstances led her to a less severe and more sensual style focused mainly on life and death. Empowered again, her palette was filled with fierce lines and dark colors creating the series "Earth Green" and "Umber", the first with extravagant images that invite birth, destruction and regeneration; the second (coinciding with a brain aneurysm she suffered) with darker and more meditated images that form bodies that seem to swell and contain the colors of the earth. Many critics saw in her work a kind of continuity with that of her deceased husband, as if she were trying to resurrect her canvases, however what she was looking for was to detach herself from him and recover her style that, for too long, had been buried. The diagonals that intersect, the arches in different directions, the raw forms were alien to Pollock's work and totally personal to Krasner, yet even though he was dead, his shadow continued to overshadow it.

When his work was being consolidated, in 1962, he suffered a stroke that took him into a picture of chronic instability as a result of which he suffered a fall that caused a fracture in his wrist. After his recovery, in 1965, he successfully exhibited his work at the Whitechapel Gallery in London and in 1973 at the Whitney Museum in New York, where he demonstrated that he had radically changed his style by opting for a flat, geometric painting in pure colours.

Krasner also applied her wisdom in marketing, projection, empowerment and inclusion in the art market by holding individual exhibitions through which she managed to disassociate herself from her husband's and be recognized with a name of her own. In addition to her work, Lena worked on the creation of the Pollock-Krasner Foundation for the promotion and dissemination of young artists, which, after years of effort, managed to establish itself in 1985, one year after his death.

Lena Krasner is one of the few living abstract expressionist women who was able to be present at a retrospective exhibition of her work at the MoMA and one of the many who ended her professional career by getting married, not being able to recover it until she buried her husband.

She died in 1984, at the age of 75. Her remains rest in Green River Cemetery in Springs along with those of Pollock. His under a large headstone, like her barn; hers in a small one, like her own room. Two worlds and two spaces that male chauvinism has hierarchized into the sexes even in death.

BAROQUE IMAGERY IN FEMININE: LUISA ROLDÁN, LA ROLDANA DE SEVILLA.

Luisa Roldán "Nuestra Señora de la Soledad". 1688. Puerto Real.

Throughout Europe, including Spain, the situation of women until very recently was one of total dependence on men. They could be married, widows, consecrated virgins, maids or prostitutes, but they always acted according to their place in the world, in a vicious or virtuous manner and always with man as their destiny.

It is difficult, therefore, to find a woman who could play a different role from the one assigned to her, and even more difficult to do it with her own name, without a pseudonym, even if the same story was in charge of stealing or hiding it. In the artistic field, specifically in sculpture, despite the fact that this brought her some fame and much poverty, we find, in the 17th century, the nicknamed Roldana de Sevilla, the first registered Spanish sculptor and creator of magnificent religious images for processions.

The Roldana was during the reigns of Charles II and Philip V chamber sculptor and signed his works adding the title, the Roldana received orders from the highest religious institutions in Andalusia. The royal house assigned an annual salary of one hundred ducats to La Roldana, which was never paid; the clergy paid La Roldana with sung masses with an answer for her soul. La Roldana died at the age of 54, having never stopped working and having made a declaration of poverty a few days before.

Luisa Ignacia Roldán Villavicencio was born in Seville in 1652, the fifth of the twelve descendants of the marriage formed by the famous sculptor Pedro Roldán and Teresa de Jesús Mena Ortega y Villavicencio. From a very young age she helped in her father's workshop so she soon learned the trade by collaborating in polychromy, carving and drawing sculptures. At the age of 19, and despite her father's opposition, she married the sculptor's apprentice Luis Antonio Navarro de los Arcos and stayed in Seville. At the age of 20 she had her first daughter, two years later her second, and so on until she gave birth to a total of 7 children. In spite of this, he never stopped sculpting. Luisa Ignacia worked in wood and clay, made small groups of devotion for individuals, terracotta nativity scenes and many images "of candlesticks" or to dress, always within the guidelines required by the Council of Trent to bring religion to the people, to humanize the art.

Luisa Ignacia's early work, when she made it in workshops, was not signed, but researches attribute to her in her Sevillian period a Virgen de la Regla that belongs to the Hermandad del Prendimiento, a Virgin of the Macarena from the brotherhood of the same name, a Virgin of the Star in which it bears the name, the Virgin of the See in the church of the Hospital de los Venerables Sacerdotes, the Virgin of Carmen, existing in the Carmelite convent of Santa Ana and the Pilgrim Virgin that is preserved in the museum of the Benedictine Mothers of the Monastery of the Holy Cross of Sahagún.

Being the mother of 4 girls and 2 boys, in 1684 the sculptor moved with her family to live in Cadiz. Her husband collaborated in her creations. In the capital of Cádiz and for its cathedral she made an "Ecce Homo" and the municipal deputies of the festivities of the Patrons of the city commissioned her to make the sculptures of "San Servando" and "San Germán". Also from his workshop are the Lord of Humiliation belonging to the Brotherhood of "La Piedad", which is located in the church of Santiago Apostle, headquarters of the Brotherhood; the images of St. John the Baptist and St. Joseph, placed on a baroque altar in the parish of St. Anthony, and for the church of the monastery of Our Lady of Mercy a group of sculptures representing a Holy Family.

At the same time that in Cadiz, the Roldana in Jerez de la Frontera worked for the Convent of Santo Domingo making the images of the Child Jesus of the Brotherhood of the Sweet Name of Jesus, for the church of San Lucas a San José, and for several brotherhoods as the one of La Oración en el Huerto and the one of El Prendimiento different processional steps as well as the one of Nuestra Señora de los Dolores for the city of San Lúcar de Barrameda.

Four years later, around 1688, Luisa Ignacia decided to move with her family to Madrid with the intention of working for the Court and obtaining official recognition. She began by doing commissions for various aristocrats who allowed her and her family to go on living. On October 15, 1692 La Roldana was appointed by Charles II as a "Chamber Sculptor", which represented her official prestige, but not the economic one as she surely expected.

The work he did was poorly paid and he even had difficulty in collecting payment, for at that time the general situation of the kingdom was bad because of poor administration and corruption. Thus, on several occasions he had to make requests for a room in the Treasury houses (where a large number of the artists of the King's Chamber lived near the Alcazar), since he had nowhere to live. Having no answers he addressed his demands to the queen to whom he asked for clothes or whatever it was convenient to give him. A letter dated in 1697 in his own handwriting said: *"because I am poor and have children, I have a very hard time because many days are lacking for the necessary sustenance of each day"*.

In spite of the calamities he continued working, from this period are the Archangel St. Michael with the devil at his feet, a work commissioned by the king to decorate the monastery of El Escorial and a relief of the Virgen de la leche in the cathedral of Santiago de Compostela, both signed and with the inscription of his position.

The death of Charles II in 1700 and the arrival of the new king, Philip V, did not bring about too many changes in the life of Luisa Ignacia, who had to ask the new monarch to renew her appointment. She presented the new king with two works, a Burial of Christ and a Nativity, asking him for *"a house to live in and a ration to support herself and her children... I put in consideration of Your Majesty, that what she knows she executes in stone, in wood, in clay, in bronze, in silver, and in any other material"*. In October of the new king he again granted her the appointment of Chamber Sculptor. From this last period are an Archangel Saint Michael in the monastery of the Descalzas Reales and six passionate angels in the Collegiate Church of Saint Isidore.

For years the work of La Roldana was attributed to her father Pedro Roldán, her husband Luis Antonio Navarro de los Arcos and other sculptors such as Juan

Martínez Montañés or Jerónimo Hernández. Today, thanks to the feminist historiography, her name is recognized as one of the most outstanding sculptors of the Spanish baroque, and some of her works are even exhibited at the Hispanic Society of America in New York.

In addition to her magnificent technique, which influenced later artists such as Pedro Duque Cornejo, Cristóbal Ramos and José Montes de Oca, La Roldana's work must be valued for the difficulties that women had in accessing the job market where she had access in patriarchal institutions such as the church and the monarchy.

Her works, charged with drama on the one hand and intimacy and serenity on the other, run through many Andalusian streets, reminding us, among other things, that the sculpture has a woman's name and that poverty is feminised, since she, after a lifetime of work, childbirth and upbringing, died declaring herself to be absolutely destitute.

THE CONFINED SPACE: WOMEN ON THE BALCONY.

Sigmund Freud said that sometimes we dream of sliding along the facades of houses, that those with smooth walls represent men and that those with projections and balconies symbolize women to hold on to. Dreams aside, the truth is that balconies and their balustrades are spaces where the feminine has been subdued for centuries because of its gender.

Since the Renaissance, the theme of women on the balcony or leaning out of a window has been painted, a composition that has been repeated throughout time and art history, varying according to the artist but maintaining its form. Another excuse to represent women, another way of stereotyping and objectifying them. Balconies and windows have allowed spectators access to the private lives of women who, oppressed behind balustrades, railings, bars or small doors, were unable to access public space.

Between 1808 and 1812 Francisco de Goya painted Maja and Celestina on the balcony, a work that belongs to a private collection. Two women appear in the work, one old, perverse, pimp; the other young, luxuriant, a prostitute. Two ages, two worlds, two stereotypes of women. The old woman in the semi-darkness, bent over, whispering; the young woman showing her cleavage and prominent bust leaning on her crossed arms and smiling, provoking the beholder.

The theme also inspired Eugenio Lucas Velázquez who, in 1862, painted the Majas on the window and is on display at the Prado Museum. Also, and behind an iron railing two women are exhibited. One plays a guitar, the other sings and in the background, many others murmur. Chubby, seductive, young bodies of women trapped on a balcony.

In 1869, the Frenchman Eduard Manet painted The Balcony that today is in the Musée d'Orsay in Paris and, following the same iconographic scheme, he depicted Berthe Morisot sitting and Fanny Claus standing behind the railing, two intellectual women who are also fenced in.

Fanny was one of Manet's favourite artists. She was 23 years old when she performed it and was already a concert violinist, member of the first women's string quartet, and married that same year the same impressionist painter and friend of the author of the work, Pierre Prins. As a result of tuberculosis, she died seven years later, at the age of 30.

Berthe was 28 years old when she was portrayed, she was one of the few women painters of the time and, despite the fact that her work is currently being revalued at that time, she was considered a second-rate artist, simply because she was a woman. A year earlier, in a letter to Henri Fantin-Latour, Manet wrote:

"The Mademoiselles Morisot are charming, it's a pity they're not men, but as women they could defend the cause of painting by marrying an academic each and thus sowing discord in the camp of these old-fashioned people, even though it would be asking too great a sacrifice of them."

Neither Fanny nor Berthe are represented as the artists they were, there is no hint of their skills. The violin that one might wear or the brushes that the other might carry are replaced by an umbrella and a fan, probably because they are more appropriate for women. However, although less talented and less recognized, standing and empowered, the artists are guarded on the balcony by Antoine

Guillemet, an impressionist painter now forgotten.

Inspired by the work of the French painter, the representative of magical realism, René Magritte, painted "Perspective II: Manet's Balcony" in 1950. This work is on display at the Ghent Museum of Fine Arts in Brussels. Magritte copied Manet's railing, gave life to the dead flowers in the Impressionist's painting with hydrangeas, and metamorphosed the characters into coffins, possibly alluding to the intrinsic death of the characters, the living death suffered by those who languish behind a balcony, the insipid contemplation of the world that is seen and cannot be felt.

Even if they have huge windows, or are wide and spacious, the balconies allow you to see possibilities, although you do not feel or touch them. You can rush or fall from one, but never caress life. For centuries, balconies and windows have been the places in the house where women have watched, barricaded and paralyzed, their hopes, where passivity became daily, where air and light penetrated the soul immobilizing the bodies, where the sounds and aromas of the street forced to take shelter, where lives were locked in the imposed privacy.

Public life began on the balconies and private life ended there. There, the female figures, who decorated them like flower pots, spoke of boyfriends, of marriages, of loves and dislikes. There they laughed, darned, gambled and made up. There they spent their days while life went away.

The whores showed off, the single ones waited for suitors and letters, the married ones sewed, the old ones whispered, the girls imitated and all of them had in common being locked up, constrained, limited.

The limited space of the balcony turned the women into gossips, gossips and pimps, their conversations, exchange of opinions and experiences into rumors and trinkets, their speculations or prognoses into bad omens, their meetings into maruisms.

This confined area, together with social insecurity, created a cultural space that was discredited by the patriarchy and whose established guidelines, norms and rules were assumed in roles that were despised, creating unhealthy legends such as the celestina, the vieja y el visillo or the Sallana, which are nothing but perverse examples built to weaken women.

FAMILY MOURNING IN THE FACE OF RAPE OR ABDUCTION: PROSERPINE AND THE SEASONS.

Ulpiano Checa "The Abduction of Proserpina".
Chinese ink, gouache, nib and gouache on paper, 59
x 44,2 cm.

Known in ancient Greece as Persephone and in Rome as Proserpina, the myth of the reborn spring and the inert winter is rooted in its history. The legend can be found in book IV of Virgil's "The Georgics", extensively recounted in the 4th century by Claudian in "De raptu Proserpinae" and mentioned by Ovid in book V of "The Metamorphoses":

"In which forests, while Proserpine

plays and rapes or lilies short,

and while with childish eagerness baskets and her breast

full and their peers struggle to overcome collecting,

almost at the same time she was seen, loved and abducted by Dis,

such was the speed of love. The goddess, terrified, with grief

mouth to his mother and his companions, but to his mother more times,

he cries out, and as from his superior shore the dress had torn,

the collected flowers on his loosened tunic fell,

and - such simplicity in his puerile years accompanied -

this loss also moved his virginal pain.

Her abductor carries the wagons and by name calls each one

urges his horses, whose neck and mane

shakes off dark rust dyeing the reins,

and by the high lakes, and by the swamps that smell of sulfur

Palicos base, boiling in the broken earth,

and where the baquiadas, the race born in Corinth, the race of two seas,

between unequal ports put up their walls. "

According to the myth, Proserpina was the daughter of Ceres and Jupiter and her charm was evident. Venus, goddess of love and mother of Cupid, sent her son to ignite love in Pluto, the lonely god of the underworld, by shooting an arrow at him. When Pluto succeeded, he was intoxicated with passion and came out of the Etna volcano with four black horses. He saw Proserpina bathing and playing in the Pergusa Lake with some nymphs while picking flowers, and without blinking he abducted her and took her to the underworld to force her, rape her and handcuff her.

Her mother Ceres (goddess of the earth), disconsolate, left in her search for all the places of the earth. In her desperation, not finding her, she stopped the growth of fruits and vegetables, refusing to return to Olympus and turning the land she was treading on into a desert. Faced with the situation, Jupiter sent Mercury to order Pluto to release Proserpine. Pluto forced him to eat six pomegranate seeds (symbol of marital fidelity) and then allowed him to march with his mother six months of the year. When Ceres met her daughter again, the fruits of the earth came out, spring began, six months later, when she was forced to return to Hades with Pluto, nature lost its colours and autumn began. In spite of the continuous violations of Pluto, Proserpina never became pregnant.

The legend of Proserpina is not only about the act of abduction, but also about the affectation to the family, the despair and death, the isolation and the return to live the aggression. When a woman is assaulted or raped, she initially suffers a phase so traumatic that she becomes depersonalized, the reality hurts so much that, to protect herself, she talks about her body in the third person. She may not even remember. Then she begins to be aware of what happened, to feel physical and emotional pain, and even to think about the irreversible damage that may have been done to her reproductive organs, including possible pregnancy and sexually transmitted diseases. The questions and the subsequent process re-victimize her, reliving what happened down to the last detail, remaining in a state of continuous alert or anxiety, avoiding situations or places associated with the rape she suffered. In Proserpina's case the cruelty is so immense that Pluto forces her to spend 6 months of the year not only remembering, but living and coexisting with him in the underworld. Metaphorically, just as she suffers isolation and emotional death, earthly nature dies. The underworld where Pluto leads her is the death of the emotions and senses.

In these situations the reaction of the family nucleus is fundamental and can lead to the decomposition of the family by blaming it or the family itself. In the case of this myth, the support of his mother Ceres, as well as the reaction of Jupiter and Mercury when they see the consequences, cause them to come to his liberation. The situation of her daughter Ceres manifests it being unable to fertilize the earth, dying the time of captivity and flourishing in his release. Proserpina's suffering is the death of her mother; her freedom, immense happiness.

The myth of this abduction has been represented by many artists, each one interpreting it in their particular style and vision. Albrecht Dürer, Niccolo dell'Abate, Joseph Heintz, Rubens, Rembrandt, Brueghel and Luca Giordano are some of them, but the one of the Spanish painter Ulpiano Checa is one of the most moving.

Born in Colmenar de la Oreja, Madrid, in 1888, in Indian ink, gouache, nib and gouache on paper, Ulpiano Checa made the "Rapto" which he presented in a medium format (59x 44.2) at the Salon des Champs-Elysées in Paris. His painting mixes key styles of the period he lived in (Orientalism, Impressionism and Romanticism), however his interpretation of the legend advances a disturbing expressionism because of its dynamism and overwhelming drama. Following the guidelines of Gericault in the drawing of the horses in movement, Ulpiano Checa anticipates the images that the cinematography of the 20th century will make films like "Quo Vadis" or "Ben-Hur", where in the circus the chariots going around the spina competed with their chariots. Ulpiano Checa proposes Pluto as a postillion in the race that, in a light two-wheeled cart pulled by four black steeds, carries Proserpina passed out in his arms. The two are the only human characters in the painting, contrasting Proserpina's white figure with Pluto's black one. The landscape is gloomy and grey, black and white submerge us in a terrifying mist that announces the end of the rapture. Pluto relentlessly whips the steeds into a gallop so that they seem to leave the painting and rush towards the viewer. Once again, Pluto's arrogance, cruelty and superiority manifest themselves as mechanisms of power against the helpless young woman. The painting is in the museum that bears his name in his hometown.

Until well into the contemporary age, the abduction of women has been a constant throughout history, firstly because they were considered sexual objects, reproductive and therefore survival of the tribe; secondly because they lacked individuality and were property. The association between kidnapping, abduction and rape has been found since ancient times, but it is not understood as a sexual aggression but as the theft of a body that is the property of a man, it has been more conceived as an ennobling and heroic act for the superior male who exercises power over the inferior, submissive and enslaved woman. The abduction is the prelude to rape, although without it it would already be a brutal manifestation of violence on the victim.

The abduction of women has been common in times of colonization, war, but also to create family alliances or arrange marriages that occurred after the attack to cover it up. The current custom of entering the wife into the bed with her arms loaded is reminiscent of abduction, which we have so assumed and normalized as well as concepts such as "the conquest" or "the triumph", all a love jargon that we should analyze.

Many of the works of art that the patriarchal culture considers as erotic art or history painting, hide blows, traumatisms and tears that in a victim cause the struggle when defending himself before a being that uses force and domination. The physical consequences of abduction or rape include menstrual disorders, miscarriages, bleeding, sexually transmitted infections, dysfunction, as well as emotional and psychological consequences such as trauma, stress, guilt, shame, isolation, suicidal thoughts and suicide.

The patriarchal culture has turned aggression into eroticism, pain into pleasure, murder into passion, slavery into power, humiliation into romance, perversion into love and works of art that should be exhibited in galleries of terror as part of passive collections of knowledge. A demonstration of the value given to the feminine.

WHEN MASCULINIZATION PREVENTS RAPE: LIBRADA FROM PORTUGAL.

Santa Librada "Sheet from the Book of Hours of Mary of Burgundy". 1477.

Hypersexualization is frowned upon, masculinization is worse. What can we women do with our bodies to integrate into society? Do we show them naturally? Do we cover them up as in the past? Whatever we do, we will be censored by society. Because we live in a society that restricts us, limits us, sanctifies us if we are chaste and objectifies us if we show off. Whatever we do, we go by word of mouth.

Sexualization is a scourge suffered exclusively by women and occurs when a person is given value only if their appearance or behavior is considered "sexy. When this happens, the woman is considered more as an object of personal satisfaction than as a human being. This leads to the objectification, depersonalization and commodification of the female body.

The latest UN figures are chilling: 750 million women were forced to marry before the age of 18, 120 million girls have been forced into sexual acts, it is estimated that half of the femicides in the world were committed by a family member or partner. These are just a few facts that show that society views women as disposable objects.

In the face of such treatment and in order to enter the public sphere or avoid being sexually abused or raped, women have been left, in most cases, with the only option of becoming masculine, aggressive, violent, competitive, and even of giving up or minimizing their sexual attributes, of going unnoticed, of being grotesque in order to avoid "that uncontrollable and masculine rape libido" that emits rude gestures, obscene words, aberrant attitudes, which intimidate, suffocate, nude and force. Men are rarely able to accept women as equals. Think of the number of women who hold high positions or are in spheres of power who dress masculinized.

Although extreme and hard to believe, but exemplary, is the legend of Librada, whose life, probably a Luso-German invention that has been transmitted in culture and art history evolving from the aspect of women to men and through sexual androgyny. A story that should make us think, taking into account the dramatization, about the pain and ordeal that women live in order to be considered equal and to avoid contempt and even sexual abuse.

Librada lived in the 8th century, she was the daughter of the king of Gallaecia and Lusitania and, from her birth, her father promised her to the Moorish king of Sicily.

Although raised in a pagan environment, Librada grew closer to Christianity until she became a Christian and decided to take a vow of chastity. As the years passed and the wedding date approached, Librada prayed and asked God to free her from this torment because she did not want to get married. She prayed for a miracle to turn her into a repulsive being but, possibly out of fear and suffering, she would fast, vomit and break her nails. It was all a consequence of the hormonal imbalance. She lost weight, her hair fell out, and hair grew all over her body including her beard. She became a hideous being so that when the Moorish king met her he rejected her and accused Librada's father of deception. This humiliated man had her crucified. It is considered that what Librada suffered was a nervous anorexia.

The cult of Librada spread throughout Europe, although under different names. Uncumber in England; Kümmernis, Kummernis or Wilgefortis in Germany; Oncommer, Ontcommer, Ontkommena, Ontcommene in the Netherlands; Múnia in Barcelona; Vierge Forte in Provence;

Eutropia in Greece; Liberata in Galicia and Italy; Livrade in France and Starosta in the Czech Republic. However, they all have in common their iconography which is the origin of the representations of Jesus dressed and crucified which is a great surprise in the interpretation of art, a masculine and powerful image in the man at the same time as grotesque and monstrous as in the woman, which makes her the bearded female circus performer.

The legend of Librada is a legend that we can transfer to reality and that reverts to those disgusting suggestions made to women, blaming them for the abuses experienced. What if that short skirt, or that tight pant, or that provocative neckline, do we women have to masculinize ourselves in order not to be sexual objects? Do we have to become unnoticed hermaphrodites in order to tame wild beasts? Is it necessary to deny our femininity in order to preserve our virginity?

A whole series of stereotypes have been created in the patriarchal society we live in, where blondes have been branded as dumb, thick ones as generous, ugly ones as smart, and pretty ones as whores. Stereotypes that, in addition to labelling and stigmatising us, have set us against each other among the same women, condemning each other, filling us with envy and competition for something so stupid.

And to top it all off, as if Librada wasn't enough, she takes the ugly ones to the altars as amulets against bad marriages or as a prayer to undo unwanted marriages. It is precisely to avoid these situations that Librada is invoked.

Bearded, crucified and with a violinist at her feet, she is the image that all over Europe has received the cult of the unfortunate, of the fearful and conscious of the weaknesses of the bodies, of the bad thoughts, of the aberrant acts, of the sexual crimes. It is free from legend and perplexity, but it is linked to the reality that women today have to live in order to be part of the spheres of power and decision making, and which necessarily involve masculinisation, bad marriages, the renunciation of motherhood or the concealment of sensitivity.

Feminizing the world is a necessary task. The idea of basing success on money, of subjugating with predatory, ambitious, aggressive and individualistic attitudes, for the good of all, must end. Capitalist and masculinized success is too serious a problem that concerns the whole of society and that is surviving ever stronger in the collective imagination.

We define people by their professions and we give them social legitimacy by the same, leaving aside those who carry out non-productive but reproductive tasks, keeping them invisible. We women are forced to choose between our jobs and our uterus, between success and care.

We women have been forced to be part of that hegemonic idea of success created from the cruelest androcentrism and that has generated an exterminating society that has underestimated the roles associated to the feminine to the point of considering them unproductive.

We can continue to renounce our femininity so as not to be devoured by a patriarchal system that oppresses and constrains us, we can stop caring for and loving each other so as not to fall into the jaws of the lions, and we can allow ourselves to be crucified for defending what we believe in and defend as Librada did. However, we can and must also feminize success, rethink and plan our lives, prioritizing values and care, cooperating and valuing others, supporting ourselves to move towards a more just society where success lies first and foremost in happiness and in building a life that deserves to be lived with intensity.

STANDARD PERVERSIONS: LOT AND HIS DAUGHTERS.

Hendrick Goltzius "Lot and His Daughters". 1616.
140×204 cm. Rijksmuseum , Amsterdam.

Nameless, naked and perverse, Lot's daughters are part of that category of witches, whores or harlots who embody evil and who oppose the virtuous models of virginity and goodness. Once again we are faced with the female dichotomy of bad-good woman.

However, what is really striking about this story is not the reality of it (certainly incredible, like so many others), but how it has served as an "excuse" for many artists to create works of art in which sexual relations between mature men and young women are normalized, for reproductive purposes, and which basically contains issues such as male sexual potency independent of age, female sexual potency strangled by various limits, the sex-reproduction bond and the justification of desire for young and adolescent women that are in reality perversions, pederasty. Reversing roles is unthinkable.

Based on the biblical passage from Genesis 19, 30-38 and the pictorial productions inspired by it, from feminism it is necessary to reflect on the social normalization that exists between adult men and young women as well as the stigma that exists in reverse. Also to meditate on the myth of reproduction in order to make invisible and justify the sexual relations and abuses that, evidently, are allowed to those of the male sex. Women, however, throughout their lives are questioned about their desires and denied with the advent of menopause and the end of reproduction when the ability to have these feelings and sex is nullified.

The legend tells the following. Displeased with the homosexual practices in the ancient city of Sodom, God revealed to Abraham that He would destroy the city by fire and brimstone, considering it a grave and irreversible sin, and that only Lot and his family could be saved. Abraham begged him not to do so and God gave him the option of finding fifty righteous people in the city, but he could not find even ten.

God sent two angels to the city to rescue Lot. His beautiful appearance caught the attention of the inhabitants, who came to Lot's house to sodomize and abuse them. The old man refused to let them pass, and offered his virgin daughters in return, to be raped and gone. The men did not accept and tried to break down the door, but the angels blinded them by giving Lot the command to take his family out of the city, without looking back. With his wife and daughters on the mountain, Edith, Lot's wife turned her head and became a pillar of salt. The old man and his daughters advanced on the road. He was the only male, so there was no possibility of descent.

Faced with this situation, Lot "for reasons of procreation and hospitality" offered his daughters to neighbouring villages to impregnate them, but they despised and rejected them. Thus, understanding that their inevitable destiny would be sterility and loneliness, the girls decided one night to get their father drunk in order to have sex and become pregnant. The same night they consumed the act. One of them conceived in Moab, from which the Moabites descended; the other conceived in Ben-Ami, the origin of the Ammonites.

The story contains all types of degenerations, especially taking into account that God considered Lot to be one of the few just men in spite of consuming incest, deceit, offering rape, covering up the myth of procreation, concealing sexual desire, etc. However, and in spite of the story, painting has shown that history is detached from it and, as a turning point, works are produced in all styles and schools where the only thing that is evident is the normalisation of sexual relations between an old man and a young woman.

Albrecht Aldorfer in 1537, Jan Massys in 1565, Ja Muller in 1600, Franchesco Furini in 1633, Rubens in 1635, Jacob van Loo in 1650 and even Gustave Courbet in 1844, among others, are painters who have produced works that are part of great museums and collections where, following the same iconography, they have propagated as normal the sexual relations between people of different sexes in which the man doubles the age, forming part of that vision of an imaginary collective that we assume with normality. Among them, one of the most disturbing is the one executed in 1616 by Hendrick Goltzius, which today is in the Rijksmuseum in Amsterdam and whose measurements are 140×204 cm.

Hendrick Goltzius is considered the best engraver in the Netherlands of Nordic Mannerism, for his sophisticated technique and the exuberance of his compositions. Coming from a humble family, at the age of 21 he married an elderly widow, thanks to whose fortune he was able to establish an independent workshop in Haarlem. Soon after, the disagreements arose and he left his country to move to Italy where he discovered the Renaissance masters. Influenced by Michelangelo's monumental figures he produced his version of "Lot and his daughters".

The scene takes place in the middle of a leafy and peaceful landscape in whose center and with the genitals covered by a red canvas is the father, without any sign of drunkenness, complacent, bearded, bald, with flabby and toasted skin that accentuates his age. At the sides his daughters, pink, smooth, young, naked and serving food and drink to their father who receives them gratefully. The image contains a grotesque naturalness that we can only understand if we reverse the roles and replace, mentally, the image of Lot with an old woman, and theirs with two ephebes. The roles and stereotypes are so accepted from the patriarchy that, being a rude scene, we have totally accepted them.

Works of art like the current media have created images where it is difficult to locate adult women and even less associated with young boys, unless of course they are their children, and even with that, we will never find them naked or with any sexual connotation. However, works and media are plagued by strong, powerful, older male images that presume to be more experienced, decisional and powerful than those of teenagers, young women and even girls with childlike bodies who are grossly abused.

Car brands, perfume ads, businesses of all kinds, sports advertising, constitute in the capitalist and consumerist media an echo of the most abominable and repugnant patriarchy that has been normalized throughout history, covered up by a false seduction and eroticism.

THE INVISIBLE AND REALISTIC BARRIERS OF MADRID.

Isabel Quintanilla "Roma", 1962. Oil on canvas. 78 x 90 cm Colección Julio Martínez y Reyes de Molina.

The patriarchal need to subjugate women in order to empower men by satisfying their needs and preventing their personal and professional growth, despite the achievements made, continues to be a reality that translates into invisible barriers but with solid foundations in our society and which prevail today. These barriers appear in different periods of life and translate into labor inequalities that are graphically described in the expressions "glass ceiling", "sticky floor", "cement ceiling" and "diamond ceiling".

The glass ceiling is an invisible barrier, difficult to cross, that describes a specific moment in a woman's professional career, in which, instead of growing because of her preparation and experience, she is stuck within a work structure, trade or sector and which, on many occasions, coincides with the stage in her life when she decides to become a mother.

This is not a legal obstacle, but rather widespread prejudices against trusting women in positions of responsibility, paying a salary and giving them a similar status for the same functions, considering that they will settle for less, as well as subtle patriarchal practices of the business world, such as the type of meetings, male corporatism or cronyism.

Sticky ground or floor refers to the tasks of care and family life to which women have traditionally been relegated. Leaving this "natural space" that according to the patriarchy corresponds to them is an obstacle to their professional development. There is a lot of pressure within the couple, in the family and in society to make women believe that they are primarily responsible for care. The feeling of guilt and the double workdays make it difficult for them to promote themselves professionally, as the male business world is configured.

The cement ceiling is the limits that women have to grow politically, socially or entrepreneurially, due to the lack of references, motherhood, personal life, greater self-criticism or a different way of understanding leadership and professional ambition. This concept has to do with sexist education, the organization of time in companies (without taking into account conciliation) or the way hierarchies are historically established in corporations. In order to overcome this ceiling, many women have the only option to adapt to male work structures, schedules and dynamics by giving up their condition as women.

The diamond ceiling is a term coined by Amelia Valcárcel in her book 'La política de las mujeres' (1997, Ediciones Cátedra) and refers to the fact that, in patriarchal society, men are an "object of appreciation" and women an "object of desire", thus subordinating them to a situation in which men perpetuate their power. The diamond ceiling prevents women from being valued on strictly professional grounds and undermines women's self-esteem in aspiring to a position of leadership.

These barriers, sometimes imperceptible, can be seen in the emergence, evolution and end of the artistic movement known as "Realistas de Madrid" formed by a group of men and women born in Spain in the 1930s and who met while studying in the 1950s. The group was made up of Isabel Quintanilla, María Moreno, Antonio López , the brothers Julio and Francisco López Hernández , Esperanza Parada, Amalia Avia and Lucio Muñoz , although the latter opted for abstract painting. It was a rather closed nucleus because, apart from family ties, the common friendship dated from the time they met. Strictly speaking, what is called a clan.

The group defended an academic but ambitious realistic painting, with a serious vocation and with the aim of showing that painting had ceased to be the avant-garde and the light of the arts, as it had been since the beginning of the 19th century. The realists did not return to the past, they tried to bring the past to the present.

Paradoxically, despite the fact that men and women had the same training and enjoyed the same prestige in their first exhibitions, getting married together with gender issues meant that they had to abandon their professional careers and devote themselves first to looking after their husbands and then their homes, then their sons and daughters and finally their elders. Nowadays we find geniuses of painting like Antonio López, and of sculpture like the brothers Julio and Francisco López Hernández, while Isabel, María, Esperanza and Amalia, because of their condition as women, were left behind in the artistic panorama.

Isabel Quintanilla was born in Madrid in 1938 and in 1953, at the age of fifteen, she entered the Escuela Superior de Bellas Artes. She successfully graduated five years later, in 1958. In 1960, Quintanilla received a scholarship to do an illustration sangria at the Beatriz Galindo Institute. It was in this student and artistic environment that he met the sculptor Francisco López, with whom he married and moved to France.

Although her husband preferred her to paint than to have a shirt ironed for her, she could hardly reconcile the upbringing of her son, the care of her sick mother staying at home, the care of the household chores and unconditional support for her husband's career so she had to abandon her dedication to painting for years. In addition, in her attempts to exhibit in France she met gallery owners who took her paintings and did not pay her, feeling that they treated her with contempt for being a woman and not considering her a painter.

With more time for her, she resumed her studies and in 1982, she graduated in Fine Arts from the Complutense University of

Madrid, starting to give drawing classes in a workshop directed by Trinidad de la Torre.

Isabel Quintanilla died in October 2017, in her residence in Brunete, leaving as a legacy a series of still lifes and oil landscapes where she demonstrated her ability to capture textures and, almost always, using diffused light.

María Moreno was born in 1930 in Madrid into a liberal family that left the capital to move to Valencia, although they soon returned to the capital of Spain. In 1954, at the age of 21, she entered the San Fernando School of Fine Arts. There she met Antonio López, whom she married in 1961, after graduating and becoming a drawing teacher.

One year after getting married, in 1962 she gave birth to the first of her daughters, María, and in 1965 to the second, Carmen. Between pregnancies, births and post births, besides care and upbringing, she continued to paint the intimate reality that surrounded her, her world conceived in corridors, stairs, interior windows, vases, flowers, still lifes, scenes of the domestic environment drawn from the window of her studio from where she observed the garden that she herself looked after. Genre painting was gaining prestige until, in 1962, she participated in the National Fine Arts Exhibition at the Palacio de Velázquez del Retiro, in 1966 she exhibited at the Edurne Gallery "Oil paintings with silence inside"; in 1973 in Frankfurt, at the Herbert Meyer-Ellinger Gallery and in 1990 in Paris, at the Claude Bernard Gallery. The gallery owner, Claude Bernard, was fascinated by his work at that time and bought it all. Years later Bernard wanted to organize another exhibition dedicated to the painting of Maria Moreno, but it was no longer possible. Maria no longer painted.

In 2016, the program dedicated to her work and titled "María Moreno, la luz de Antonio" was broadcasted on channel 2 of TVE, alluding to the fact that she was the wife of the second most internationally quoted Spanish artist.

Esperanza Parada was born in San Lorenzo del Escorial on February 18, 1928 and in

Madrid she began her career as a painter at the Peña Academy, where she was then preparing to enter the School of Fine Arts. In the forties she completed her practice of natural drawing at the Círculo de Bellas Artes in Madrid where she met her husband, the sculptor Julio López Hernández, in 1962. Before getting married, in 1957, she held her first exhibition at the Sala Macarrón in Madrid, the only private gallery that exhibited the artists of her time. In the 1960s, she made medals and small-format reliefs that were exhibited both in Spain and abroad on commission from the Fábrica Nacional de Moneda and exhibited at the Juana Mordó Gallery. However, when she married and had two daughters, Marcela and Esperanza, she decided to devote herself to her family life and to prioritise her husband's work above her own. Her pictorial activity was practically abandoned until the 90's, when she was more liberated from her family occupations, she took up painting again and participated in several collective exhibitions, always linked to the group of Madrid realists. Thus, in 1992 she participated in the exhibition Otra Realidad. Compañeros in Madrid and in 2002 in the exhibition Nocturnos y Luz de la Mirada. He died in Madrid on 30 January 2011 and in 2016 his work was displayed at the Thyssen Museum in the relevant exhibition dedicated to the group of Realist painters and sculptors who had lived and worked in Madrid with the título: Realistas de Madrid.

Amalia Avia was born in Santa Cruz de la Zara, province of Toledo, in 1930, moving to Madrid where she trained with the painter Eduardo Peña and later entered the San Fernando Academy of Fine Arts, where she met her husband, Lucio Muñoz, also an artist, whom she married in 1960. The couple got to know each other both artistically and personally. Amalia, a realist, and Lucio, an abstract, had adjoining studies and were a support to each other. In spite of being both great artists, with radically different styles and nothing comparable, Amalia was always relegated to the condition of "woman of the artist", an unfair label in which the mistake is to have assumed one genius over another. Getting married meant being relegated to the domestic space where she tried to continue working although with a tense stillness and an uncomfortable languor. Thus she dedicated herself to painting scenes that reflected the burdens of housework, complaining in pictorial form and expressing her rebelliousness about it. Despite the fact that her husband Lucio helped her with the chores, the responsibility for the house and the care of the family was exclusively for her, so she had to give up her professional career while helping to strengthen that of her husband, who, with a linear time, dedicated all the time he needed to paint. The upbringing of her son Diego deprived her of the time to devote to her work, remaining practically twelve years without activity. She had to wait until 1972 to exhibit in the Biosca Gallery where she presented herself as a "painter of absences" whose tremendously human themes were inspired by squares, shops, corners and still lifes. Amalia painted what she could not photograph.

In 1978 she was awarded the Goya Prize of the Villa de Madrid. In 1992 a great exhibition was held ("Another reality. Partners in Madrid") about the group of friends, both realistic and abstract, that emerged around the San Fernando Academy of Fine Arts.

In 1997 he held a large anthological exhibition at the Centro Cultural de la Villa de Madrid and was awarded the Medal of Artistic Merit by the City Council. In the eighties he also started to work in interiors. To her work on board we must add a long trajectory as an engraver.

In 2004 she published her memoirs De puertas adentro, with notable success in the art world.

Camilo José Cela wrote about her work, who said of Amalia Avia that she was the painter of absences, the bitter chronicler of the "here she spent her life marking her bitterness and inevitable trace of pain".

She died on 30 March 2011 in Madrid. Today she is remembered with a paper relegated as a painter member of the group "Realistas de Madrid"

Isabel Quintanilla, María Moreno, Esperanza Parada and Amalia Avia, the Realistas de Madrid are a clear example of the opacity of the feminine in the face of the masculine, of the conversion of workers into caregivers, of independents into dependents, of painters into muses, of renunciation, of invisibility. Lights, shadows and shooting stars that disappear in the face of male hegemony.

AMONG THE TILES AND POTS: THE STILL LIFES.

Claude Raguet "A Gentleman's Table". 1897. Oleo sobre lienzo. 45,7 x 81,2 cm. Private collection.

As a reflection of life itself, many women artists confined to the domestic sphere have dedicated themselves to capturing on their canvas those objects that were close to them, that were part of their daily lives and that allowed them to continue with the practice of painting without neglecting the tasks that society had imposed on them: staying at home, taking care of their children, caring for the sick and isolating themselves from public, social and working life.

Among crockery, cutlery, jars, food and fruit, they discovered the possibility of continuing with their painting practices through objects close to them, within their reach and, with them, perfecting their technique, experimenting with curves and lines, making mixtures and becoming experts in a type of painting that, perhaps because it is generally female, is considered low level, marginalized and relegated by portrait, landscape, religious or historical scenes. However, and even more curious, although it is standardised in the patriarchal discourse, both textbooks and museums and art manuals exhibit glorious still lifes of Velázquez, Zurbarán, Caravaggio or any other well-known master of universal painting, ignoring and making invisible the real experts in the field who are the still lifes.

The number of women artists who have cultivated this pictorial genre is innumerable, however, one of the perhaps best known is that of Clara Peeters, by the way, the first woman around whom the

Prado Museum has held an exhibition, which took place in 2016. Clara is considered the initiator of this genre in the Netherlands.

She was born in Antwerp in 1594 and as a peculiarity of her work she painted herself with miniatures in the decorations and stones of jars and plates she painted. She was the author of breakfast and flower scenes in which precious metal or ceramic objects, which apparently accumulated in disorder next to flowers, fruits and pieces of fishing or hunting, created a multicoloured ensemble. She was also very skilled at distinguishing textures. Peeters' work stands out for its elegance, with a total of only 31 signed canvases such as Clara Peeters or Clara P., other paintings with the PC anagram and some unsigned ones that have also been attributed to her, produced between 1607 and 1621. Clara managed to get the Holladay couple, art collectors, to take a liking to her work, which was exhibited in a gallery in Vienna and later in the Prado Museum. Peeters' art encouraged the couple to create a space in which to give prominence to women artists from all over the world and of all times. Thus, in 1987 the National Museum of Women in the Arts, NMWA, was born, which currently has more than three thousand paintings, sculptures and other artistic pieces created by women. Its database was named Clara, after its inspirer, Clara Peeters.

Also of great interest is the work of French painter Anne Vallager, born in Paris in 1744 and considered the most important in this genre of her time. At least 400 works are recorded of her, with themes of flowers, hunting, musical instruments, military trophies, kitchen utensils, luxurious porcelain, hams, lobsters, fruits, in small or large paintings and compositions made with a technique so refined and realistic that it incites the viewer to approach and check if the images are real.

Her talent led her to be unanimously elected a member of the Royal Academy of Art in Paris. She was protected from Queen Marie Antoinette and during the French Revolution she did not stop painting because her themes, which were not very politically committed, allowed her to continue with her art after the turbulent years. Anne painted many pictures of flowers of great modernity, her painting is of thin layers. Because of their subject matter, containing silverware or military trophies, they brought her closer to an aristocratic audience.

In the United States, at the end of the 19th century and until the middle of the 20th century, the figure of Claude Raguet stands out, who was also acclaimed for using the trompe-l'oeil technique. She was born in Cincinnati, Ohio in November 1855 and began her painting classes at the age of ten. At the age of 14 she was enrolled in the Mount Auburn Young Ladies Institute and, when she was only 17, in 1872, the Cincinnati Industrial Exhibition included three of her first works.

The themes of her early New York still lifes included fruits and flowers, mostly pansies and roses, and she often identified the varieties of roses in her titles. During the 1880s, however, she began to use a male iconography, creating what became known as "still lifes" in which she incorporated elements such as books, candles, newspapers, and sea foam pipes arranged on a wooden table. He therefore abandoned flowers as a theme and spent the rest of his career focusing on library tabletop compositions. Claude Raguet managed to get this masculinized version of the still life acquired for offices, cafes, restaurants and other more visible public spaces. In "A Gentleman's Table", pipes, bottles, glasses and cards are arranged on a table. The work was commissioned by a men's club in Chicago and offers a subtle critique of men's gambling and drinking activities. It can be seen that most of the bottles are empty, suggesting that a lot of alcohol has been consumed, the sugar cubes and lemon slices indicate that one of the liquors is absinthe, considered the cocaine of the 19th century, the overturned bottles, the cards scattered on the table and the abandonment of a pyramidal composition create a feeling of disorder at work. Everything is calculated with a moralistic intention.

At the same time, and in Spain, Adela Ginés, a student at the San Fernando School of Fine Arts in Madrid and later a teacher at the Association for the Teaching of Women, began painting vases and finally specialized in still lifes where she combined fruit and foliage with roosters and small birds.

Her paintings on religious themes have been exhibited in churches and temples that are a must for everyone; her paintings on history have won prizes and awards and have been exhibited in institutions and museums; her portraits and landscapes have been exhibited in large rooms, receptions, halls and where still lifes have been located, curiously in women's spaces, kitchens, small rooms, corners, in the same hidden cubicles where women have remained and where their mastery and genius have once again been made invisible.

THE HAPPY PROSTITUTES AND THE SEX WORK.

Kees Van Dongen, "Prostitute" 1908

Victims of white slave trade in most ways, or rape in others, prostitutes are blinded by the light of day as they get used to spending their lives living in the darkness of night or lit by the red neon lights of magnifying glasses. Their "no" doesn't count, because they are whores and putting up resistance is worse, they need to stay still without complaining.

Extorted by their pimps, they abandon their beds when it begins to get dark, make up their faces with thick brushstrokes that cover their sadness and dark circles under their eyes and, with the most disheveled clothes, they get into a taxi that picks them up and leaves them on the road until dawn. In the street begins the race to be the most whore among the whores and thus obtain more privileges and recognition before his owner and lord who, of collection remains a 75%.

The clients, the whoremongers, enjoy if they see them crying and in exchange for a few miserable euros they appropriate their bodies allowing themselves to demand all kinds of aberrations, forcing them to make fellations, urinate or defecate in them, practicing the hardest of the sexes and saying goodbye saying "you are only a whore".

The most fortunate have the shelter of the roof of a club, which is visited daily by married men or men with a partner after their working day, where they wait, accustomed to suffering, violence and not feeling. There they drink, take drugs and uninhibitedly get sex in exchange for money. Young people come in droves with the aim of becoming the protagonists of the pornographic films they are used to seeing. Then there are the forty and fifty year olds who seek to prove their manhood and virility to others, who pay for violence and return home with a clear conscience to have done so in exchange for a few coins. There are also lonely, weird people who hate women and channel that hatred through prostitution. This group includes the reapers, for whom women are objects in their service; the risk-takers, who demand sex without protection, without condoms and generally accompanied by cocaine; the partner-seekers or rescuers, who seek an affective relationship that always ends in gender violence; the personalizers, who in addition to sex look for the psychologist in the woman and, ultimately, the aggressors, who resort to sex to exercise violence on women, in this case prostitutes.

Neither of them see the person behind the prostitute and, most shocking of all, they dare to say that it is "sex work" that must be legalised. Even today we are faced with the depraved idea of creating unions that seek to consider prostitution as a way out for women to work and, therefore, whoremonger pride as a new business.

Etymologically from the late Latin "burdus", which means bastard, comes brothel which, together with brothels, "mancebías" and "lupanares", have been inspiring scenarios for many artists who, in groups or alone, have conveyed to us images of happy prostitutes close to the stereotype of the femme fatale and in which, if men appear, they are reflected as passive, waiting and relaxed near the bar. These images are therefore totally at odds with reality, since they are the object and the sexual victim.

With more or less subtlety the history of art, museums and collections are plagued by these representations that make us think how attractive it must have been for the "great masters" to visit these places and how enigmatic these women were to them. Perhaps the one who quickly comes to mind is the Frenchman Toulouse-Lautrec, described by some as the friend of whores and the son of a marriage between two first cousins from an aristocratic family. A product of inbreeding, Henri was a sickly and weak boy who, when he was ten years old, began to develop a disease that affected his bones. This, added to the fact that at the age of 14 he stumbled and fractured his left femur and soon after broke his right one, caused his legs not to grow again, although the rest of his body did. His deformity, which was evident, caused him serious problems and trauma.

Since he was a child he always showed interest in art, his parents separated and he was despised by his father. He left Albi, his city of birth, at the age of 17 and moved to live in Paris where, in addition to studying drawing, he began to frequent the atmosphere of Montmartre and to interact in the cafés and cabarets with bohemians, prostitutes, absinthe and opiates, as well as painting the themes that made him famous, the brothels and whorehouses whose protagonists appear shameless, funny, frivolous, in rude attitudes that seemed to provoke in the artist sympathy and inspiration.

Through his production, Lautrec offers us an image far removed from the world of prostitution, which he makes up by turning what is really a hellhole into a circus, of which he himself ended up being a victim. A regular at the Moulin Rouge, the Jardin de Paris or the Divan Japonaise, the nightlife, bad eating, excessive alcohol and bad sleep, he devoted his last years to painting in exchange for sexual favours, food or accommodation. A paranoid crisis led him to a methylene suicide attempt, he contracted syphilis, suffered attacks of delirium tremens and finally, in 1901, at the age of 36, he died after having spent the last two years in his mother's care.

Otto Dix, José Gutierrez Solana, Rudolph Bergando, Picasso, Jean-Louis Forain or Botero are other artists among many, who, with joy, lightness and lightness have treated in their paintings the "happy" lives of the prostitutes selling an image far from reality and masking in a patriarchal key a terrifying underworld of sexual violence for women who, by force, are submitted to live from it.

Unlike them, the Dutchman, born in Rotterdam in 1877, Cornelius Théodorus Marie van Donge, with a special sensitivity captured the sad soul of these women. Signing his works as Kees van Dongen, he began his training at the Royal Academy of Fine Arts in his home town and, at the age of 16, began to frequent the dark corners of the port to rub shoulders with sailors and prostitutes. Settling in France later, and influenced by the Impressionists, Fauvists and Expressionists, he created a personal style that advocated pure, strident colours, non-submission to traditions and the non-softening of images, as well as exposing and denouncing the excesses of Montparnesse through the representation of vices, stories, characters and cruel realities.

Without any erotic or sensual charge, but quite the opposite, and with great subjectivity, Kees van Dongen portrayed prostitutes in their sickly reality, wrapped in screaming reds and features marked by thick lines of make-up that, despite the thick layers of paint, do not cover up the sadness or dark circles under the eyes.

Provocative images that, with submission and abnegation, offer their breasts to the highest bidder. Sophisticated images, with provocative clothes that show the sad reality of those "happy" prostitutes that whoremongers and pimps want to sell us and that from feminism and the fight for equality we must abolish since nothing excuses or justifies the commodification of a woman's body.

FEMININE TIMES, CIRCULAR TIME: BERTHE MORISOT.

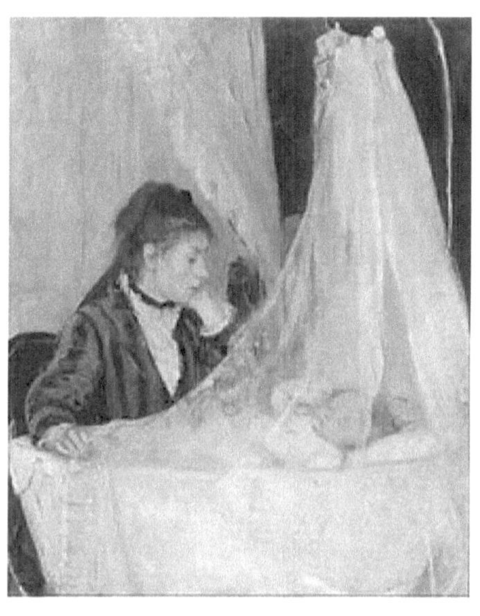

Berthe Morisot "The Cradle". 1872. Oil on canvas. 56 x 46 cm. Musée d'Orsay.

The fantasy of equality ends with motherhood. Empowered, educated, independent women with consolidated professional careers see their house of cards fall apart when they become pregnant and their life project, as a result of the macho education they have received, changes radically and forever, having to make work compatible inside and outside the home, making their time circular, combining production and reproduction, and finally giving up their dreams, since, obviously, women are not machines. In addition, society will consider her better if she renounces her work project than if she renounces her care work.

In linear time, there is a beginning and an end, an hour for entering work and an hour for leaving it, without interruptions, with total involvement, presence and concentration. With pregnancy, as the belly grows, the perception also increases that everything a woman does is impregnated by the female role that is imposed on her, and that this freedom to move around ends up where the umbilical cord begins. That living being developing in our womb wakes us up in the macho world, in which we still have the duty to care, to rock, to comfort, to breastfeed, to love unconditionally. Being a mother is revealed as the first and most important job, any other task or position that we occupy at work or socially becomes subordinate to motherhood. Thus, when women become mothers, they are forced to give up many things that a man is not obliged to give up, including his other identities. It is seen as natural and necessary that she devotes most, if not all, of her time to raising the baby, something that is taken for granted and not even valued as the great socio-economic asset that is all the reproductive work that women contribute free of charge by default. Women's times change and, without having a beginning or an end, they go to their jobs, with the bulk of the domestic burden, asking for permission to go to school tutorials, to medical appointments, taking advantage of the time off to do the shopping and, at the end of the working day, to take care of the housework. This is an exhausting circular time, which diminishes health and makes complete dedication and professional promotion impossible. The myth of a mother's love, as a supposed biological instinct, together with the myth of romantic love, has meant a slavery for women to the tasks of care and to the renunciation of their own essence in order to give all the attention to men.

In the artistic field, as in so many others, we find brilliant women painters whose motherhood brought about a radical change in their professional projection, depriving us, society in general, of the enjoyment of the wonders that women could have created and which have not been able to do so because of a patriarchal culture that has prevented it.

It is true that at the present time, with all kinds of household appliances and even with magnificent cases of couples who practice joint responsibility, women continue to feel, due to social pressure, responsible for domestic tasks and care, dedicating our time to it in a circular fashion, without having time for leisure and always being tired. Betty Friedan in "The Mystique of Femininity" of 1963 explained the phenomenon of the existential void that women feel when after studying a career or having a job they abandon it to dedicate themselves to the tasks of the house, even of the privation that they feel for feeling deprived of a function in the society according to their capacity. Therefore, banished from an active role in society, they become more bored and prolong the repetition of tasks, the monotony in their lives, the isolation and the lack of stimuli. Friedan even warned that the more intelligence exceeds the needs of work, the greater the boredom.

As Virginia Woolf already claimed in 1929 with respect to having "A room of their own", Friedan also qualifies the lack of privacy and the lack of spaces in the home where women can think, work, study or simply be alone, but he concludes that if they had them, because of the education received oriented towards dependence and care, they would not know what to do with them either and that they would use them to make them compatible with care, taking up again the idea of circular time.

The life of many women serves as an example of everything I have said, but I will exemplify it by dealing with the life of the French painter Berthe Marie Pauline Morisot, founder, key figure and fundamental exponent of the French impressionist movement, although she is invisible because she is a woman. Born in Bourges in 1841, at the age of 23 she already exhibited at the Paris Salon and in 1874, at the age of 33, in the Impressionist exhibitions together with Monet, Degas and Renoir. Berthe strove to capture the sensations of vision through a complex network of broken brushstrokes that placed her in the vanguard of her time. Her painting, closely linked to her own life and that of the people around her, showed her surroundings as she saw them, with great naturalness. Because of her talent and ability, she won the respect and public recognition of her contemporary male colleagues, an unusual achievement for the women of the time. Her willingness to break with tradition, the transcendence of her models and her ability make her the great lady of painting.

Initiated in the landscape painting that she cultivated from nature, she spent long hours at the Louvre copying the works of the great masters and learning from them until she became a prodigy of portraits. Her friendship with Édouard Manet, who later became her husband, allowed her to learn first-hand about the primordial debates on modern art and everyday reality, which used to be discussed at the Café Guebois, a place forbidden to women. Thanks to the conversations she had with this and other artists on Tuesday evenings at her family's home, and on Thursdays at Manet's, Berthe was able to get closer to the artistic circles of the time, aligning her interests with those of the future impressionist group and beginning to paint themes of domestic affairs of modern life that showed her mastery of painting in the open air. Later, coinciding with the pregnancy and maternity of her sister Edma, she provoked feelings that led her to feel attracted to themes related to family life, interior scenes, intimate meetings and maternity wards, whose work "The Cradle" of 1872 is one of the masterpieces of French Impressionism.

It is a small format oil painting, barely fifty centimetres high and a little more than forty-five centimetres wide, in which she represents her sister looking candidly at her daughter, Blanche, who has just been born, while the little girl sleeps peacefully in her crib. This is an intimate scene set in a bedroom; the mother appears seated and dressed in a black dress that stands out from the rest of the composition. One of her arms rests on the baby's crib while the other remains bent over holding her face, this posture emphasizes the diagonal of her gaze that she directs towards her daughter and that will be the axis on which the artist articulates the composition. For his part, the baby rests quietly in the crib covered with white sheets and a canopy that demonstrates the skill of the painter in the treatment of transparencies, so that, after an endless number of glazes we can see the baby's face with his eyes asleep. Edma's gesture, which runs the curtain of the crib between the spectator and the baby, further intensifies the feeling of intimacy and protective love expressed in the painting. Morisot's canvas is currently in the Musée d'Orsay in Paris. When the oil painting was finished, this type of scene became the painter's favourite.

In 1874 she married Manet and in 1878, at the age of 37, Berthe gave birth to her daughter Julie, which meant a drastic change in her pictorial production, making her a favourite model from her childhood to her adolescence. She represented her alone, with her cat, playing, sitting, standing, with her father, with a boat, with her doll, in the woods, in the bathroom and in all the postures and attitudes she could imagine. For Berthe, her motherhood did not cancel her out artistically, but it did change her way of understanding life and painting, making her daughter the epicentre of it. When Julie was only 17, her mother died from a lung congestion. Berthe Morrisot was only 54 when she died. She left us a legacy of masterpieces of the first line of French impressionism and shows the production of a professional painter, wife and mother whose motherhood not only changed her life, but also her pictorial production, time and space that was reduced to the attention of her daughter, making her her muse.

Patriarchy has turned motherhood into a myth that pressures women by limiting and oppressing them, idealizing a state that implies renouncing life projects that are alien to the biological ones. Biology,

education or the need to revive the myth
in order to maintain male supremacy?
That is.

THE FEMININE CORNERS AND THE MASCULINE UNIVERSE: ANDREY REMNEV'S SPACES.

Andrey Remnev "Untangling the Hair" 1997. 254 x 254 cm.

The differentiation between the occupation of space in the public and private spheres between men and women is an issue that needs to be reflected upon, as well as analysed in terms of urban spaces, sports practices conditioned by spaces, postures, composure and stillness in sexual relations, etc. Doing so will make us aware of how, at the same time that today women continue to be cornered, occupying a circumscribed space, they are allowed to be the owners of the universe. And this is not part of the past, nor of history, but it is a current reality that we can discuss around the work of the contemporary Russian painter Andrey Remnev, a rising superstar in the current art scene.

The incorporation of women into the public sphere has meant their introduction into a patriarchal and masculinized society and working world. Neither their needs, nor their rights, nor their reproductive or caring role have been taken into account in the modification of these spaces, so that women, in order to integrate, have had to become masculine, and therefore we must continue to talk about inequality or false equality. Women have had access to these public-labour spaces, but these spaces have not been transformed to have a reference subject other than men as a universal model. Women are incorporated into the workplace but without a change in the conception of work or in their time or in their clearly male biased relationships, to the detriment of the care for life that is originally female. This makes family responsibilities or the ability to give birth disadvantageous in the world of work, creating a female incorporation into the workplace but in an unequal situation. This means that women's relationship with the world of work continues to be an incomplete one.

As for the private sphere, the incorporation of women into the public sphere has not been accompanied by a redistribution of domestic work either, which continues to fall on women. There is no break with the sexual division of labour or patriarchal exploitation. While men do not produce domestic work, and women with studies have uninhabited the private-domestic space to move their centre of life to the public-labour space, unable to assume the domestic burden, this brings about the need to create another new subject to inhabit the private domestic space and do the work of the home. Although both spouses of the family have moved their centre of life to the public-work space, the family continues to need someone to carry out the reproductive tasks necessary for life in the private-domestic space. Consequently, the phenomenon that is occurring in the family is that the modern educated woman has abandoned her social role as a woman to adopt a male social role in a masculinized public-labour space.

In the urban spaces we find a very enlightening example that are the parks and school areas where most of the spaces are destined to extensive areas where to practice football, sport in spite of the attempts of women, masculinized and that prevents the girls to enjoy being forced to occupy corners and to avoid balls. Another abysmal imbalance.

Sports are also clear evidence of the different education that, even today, men and women receive (and of course there are exceptions, but I address the issue in general). Both at school and in out-of-school time, children play football, basketball, volleyball, sports that allow them to wear loose and baggy clothes, comfortable shoes, jump, run, dishevel, sweat and, especially, have fun in groups, create brotherhood and complicity. In contrast, girls are still taken to ballet, rhythmic gymnastics, synchronized swimming or similar sports that require strong discipline, controlled attitudes, careful and meditated hairstyles, martyrizing shoes, indoor practices, isolation and containment. Girls' leisure time has nothing to do with fun. Their spaces are again limited.

And even in the postures and composure of women we are educated limited in space. While they are allowed, and turned into macho men, to walk as if they were riding a horse, we are required to do so with our legs together. The same thing happens when sitting down, a man with his legs open shows his virility; a woman with her thighs attached, better yet tilted, her femininity which, in reality, translates into the starting point, the cornering, the occupation of the minimum space. The raised and open arms in men symbolize leadership and power, but when a woman does this she is branded as vulgar and ordinary. How elegant and angelic are the women with their arms half crossed, stuck to the body and their legs joined! What an example of domesticity!

In sex also quiet, lying down, prostrate and adopting the basic posture of the missionary, where receptive or not we endure that we face, so that, with open legs we penetrate vaginally or anally. On the contrary, we would become the fatal woman that Lilith was, who because she did not accept it, abandoned Adam.

It may be that for someone, what I have argued seems to be remnants of a past that has been overcome but, in addition to being a current and habitual reality, we find that through the media and art, this closed image of women is what is spread and socially liked, considering the opposite to be unpleasant and even "unnatural", since what is natural, in the middle of the 21st century, and for women, continues to be reclusion, limitation, compliance and abnegation. It is precisely the Russian painter Andrey Remnev, cultivating this type of image, who is becoming one of the

168

most sought-after and praised living painters in the world, and among many, the most applauded of his works "Desenredo del cabello" (Disentangling the Hair) which he executed in 1997 and whose protagonist is considered to be among the most beautiful faces in the history of art.

Andrey Remnev was born in Yakhroma, a small town outside Moscow, in 1962. His work is strongly influenced by traditional Russian icons because Remnev began his education by studying icon painting at the Holy Andronie Monastery in Moscow, home to countless Russian Orthodox works of art, many of which were painted by the abbey's most famous monk and artist, Andrei Rublev (1360-1427). Remnev combines the old with the new in his own unique style to create a statement about our modern world. According to the artist "My paintings are distinguished by attention to detail and meticulous decoration, in a traditional Russian style". Remnev's work seems very traditional initially with the dresses and costumes worn by his characters, but upon closer inspection, you can see elegant additions that propel the piece into the contemporary era. Women play an important role in Remnev's paintings giving them a universal quality of grandeur and mystery. The artist himself explains, "My characters are not real women, but symbols," creating a kind of eternal beauty and returning it to its proper status.

In "Untangling the Hair", with a quattrocentric taste, pre-Raphaelite echoes, Art Nouveau shades and constructivist touches, he presents us with that ideal of beauty that still survives in the most rancid patriarchy: young, angelic, in an enclosed and isolated space where Byzantine angels guard like a bent adult woman makes a braid in which she inserts a red cord, a cord that the young woman keeps between her hands to adorn the one on the other side. The protagonist, complacent and cornered in space, maintains a posture, like a geisha, very uncomfortable so that her hairstyle is perfect, so much so that it keeps her immobilized to appear to be a lady.

Past styles, androcentric mentalities, objectified bodies, claustrophobic enclosures, idealized beauties, non-existent canons, forced postures, images at the service of the voyeuristic male, once again raze to the ground the demands and needs of women, returning them to the corner so that the owner of the universe may once again be the male.

WOMEN AND WAR: THE IGNORED AND THE WORK OF KÄTHE KOLLWITZ.

Käthe Kollwitz "The Survivors". 1923. Käthe-Kollwitz Museum in Berlin.

When you begin to learn about history in primary education, you discover that it is full of heroes, wars, struggles, winners and losers. The Punic Wars, the conquests of the Roman people, the Visigoths and their world, the feudal lords, Al-Andalus, the discovery of America, the Napoleonic

173

Wars, the First and Second World Wars, the Spanish Civil War are studied up to high school.

Unfortunately a history of winners at the cost of murder, torture, domination that pushes them to grow and believe in a society based on these values as models to imitate to succeed. A story that shows that the winner is the one who kills and that cruelty is the banner of the champion. The story, so told, in addition to transmitting erroneous values in education and training, makes half of the population, women, the hidden and greatest victims in war conflicts, invisible.

Women have been involved in wars since they were fought. And they have done so actively, intervening by participating in combat, resisting or instigating, or opposing by denouncing, protesting or boycotting. However, historical accounts often omit the presence of women in conflicts and armies, because they were often relegated to subordinate roles and positions. Even when they were protagonists they were deliberately condemned to oblivion, when in fact they participated fully and directly in the conflicts. Supporting men or opposing them, in combat or in the rear.

Although the civilian population is often the main target of hostilities, particularly in armed conflicts, women are generally the most heavily affected victims, and there are several different types of women who take part in hostilities, women as members of the civilian population, sexual violence in armed conflicts, missing and widowed persons, displaced women, women in detention and mothers who are heads of household because, when men are fighting, they are the ones who ensure the survival of the family and the community.

Women who take part in hostilities have been active participants in armed conflicts throughout history. It was during the Second World War that their role was highlighted, primarily as reservists or support units (including work in munitions factories) in the German and British forces; in the case of the Soviet Union, their direct participation in the struggle as members of all services and units amounted to 8% of the total armed forces. Since then, women have taken on a much greater role and are more often entering the armed forces, voluntarily or involuntarily, where they assume both support and combat roles. Women are the preferred choice of lay groups when it comes to infiltration and attack missions. In the first place, women arouse less suspicion. Second, in conservative societies in the Middle East and South Asia, women are hesitant to be searched. Thirdly, women can hide a suicide device under their clothes and give the appearance of being pregnant. Women are as capable as men of committing acts of extreme violence. Women also "actively" support their partners in military operations by providing them with the moral and physical support needed to fight the war, such as cooking, caring for them, and anything else needed.

On the other hand, there are women who are at risk because of their presence among the armed forces, but who are there absolutely against their will, abducted to provide sexual services or to cook and clean the camp. During the period of their abduction, and often afterwards, these women and girls may be at considerable risk from attacks by the opposing forces, as much as their abductors. Other women are subject to suspicion and, because of the real or perceived role of their partners, are targeted for attack and intimidation in order to obtain information to reach them.

Despite these examples of women's voluntary and involuntary participation in armed conflict, either as combatants or in support roles, some countries and cultures refuse to accept women's participation in combatant roles in their armed forces. Most women experience the effects of armed conflict as part of the civilian population.

Women as members of the civilian population are victims of countless acts of violence during situations of armed conflict. They often suffer the direct or indirect effects of combat, endure indiscriminate bombing and attacks, and lack food and other items essential for healthy survival. Invariably, women have to take greater responsibility for their children and elderly relatives, and often for the wider community, when male members of the family are engaged in combat, or are interned or detained, missing or dead, internally displaced or in exile. The very fact that many of their companions are absent accentuates the insecurity and danger for women and children who have been abandoned and exacerbates the breakdown of traditional support mechanisms on which the community has relied. Due to increased insecurity and fear of attack, women flee with their children. It is well known that the majority of the world's refugees are women and children. However, many women do not flee the fighting because they and their families believe that simply being women (often with children) will protect them more from the warring parties. They believe that their gender will protect them. Thus, women often stay behind to look after their families' property and livelihoods; to look after family members, whether old, children or sick, who cannot flee because they are less mobile; to keep their children in school; to visit and support family members in detention; to search for their missing relatives; and even to assess the level of insecurity and danger, in order to decide whether their displaced relatives can return safely. However, this perception of protection does not correspond to reality. On the contrary, women have been targeted precisely because they are women.

Women are often directly threatened by indiscriminate attacks because of the proximity of the fighting. They are also forced to shelter and feed soldiers, thereby exposing themselves to the risk of reprisals by opposing forces, who are forced into difficult situations, another mouth to feed with scarce resources, and subjected to threats to their personal safety and that of their children. Because of the proximity of the fighting and/or the presence of the armed forces, women are always forced to restrict their movements; this severely limits their access to water, food and medical care and their ability to care for their animals and crops, to exchange news and information and to seek support from the community or family.

Limited access to medical care can have a huge impact on women, especially in terms of reproductive and material health. Complications from childbirth, which are more likely under the stressful conditions of war, can lead to increased infant and maternal mortality or illness. All too often women are harassed, intimidated and attacked in their homes, or when they move around in and around villages, or pass through checkpoints. Lack of identity documents seriously affects women's personal security and freedom of movement, increasing the risk of abuse, including sexual violence.

Sexual violence in armed conflict, rape, forced prostitution, sexual slavery and forced pregnancy are violations of international humanitarian law and are now an undisputed part of the vocabulary of war. They are historical crimes, but it has been taught that rape can be justified as a method of warfare or a show of power, as a reward for the victorious army or as a lesson for the vanquished who failed to protect their women.

In many conflicts, women have been systematically targeted for sexual violence, sometimes with the broader political objective of ethnically cleansing an area or destroying a village. It is not possible to give more than estimated data on the number of victims of sexual violence since many of the victims do not survive and most of them never report the rape they suffered. Reliable statistics are not easy to obtain and those that are available are often based on figures on victims who sought medical help for pregnancy, sexually transmitted diseases or childbirth. Generally, statistics are extrapolated from the figures on women seeking this type of assistance. In general, however, many women are too afraid to talk about their experiences, due to a real fear of ostracism or revenge from their family or community. Many of them also believe that after being raped no one can help them.

The very fact that many women survive conflicts in which their partners have died or disappeared has enormous consequences. Women are desperately trying to find out what happened to their loved ones. Survivors of war struggle to cope not only with the difficulty of obtaining immediate sustenance or livelihoods for themselves and their families, but also with the additional trauma and uncertainty of not knowing what will happen to them in the absence of their male relatives. Widows and relatives of missing men - fathers, sons and husbands - may well lose all their rights to land, homes and inheritance, to social welfare and pensions, or even the right to sign contracts. Because of their situation, they and their daughters may be victims of violence and ostracism.

In wars, tens of thousands of women search for the fate of their missing relatives, a search that often continues beyond the end of the conflict. The inability to mourn and bury their loved ones has an enormous impact on the survivors and the mechanisms they adopt to cope with their situation. Women are forced to show immense courage and resilience as survivors and as heads of households, a role for which many were unprepared or had little training, and which is made even more difficult by the constraints imposed. Many women have taken up this challenge and, with determination, have set aside their trauma in order to continue living for their children.

Women and children make up the majority of the world's refugees and displaced persons. Fleeing and living as displaced persons creates many problems and, ironically, exposes them to enormous risks. Women generally flee with very little property, and many are separated from their families. Displacement may well force women to rely on the support of local populations in the areas to which they have been displaced. They often have to travel long distances in search of water, food, firewood or traditional herbs and food products as medicine for themselves and their families. During this search, women are often at risk of being attacked and injured as a result of the fighting or unexploded ordnance, as well as being sexually abused, particularly rape.

Women show tremendous strength and resourcefulness in the coping mechanisms they adopt to ensure their own and their families' survival. However, women in IDP camps are often vulnerable, especially when they are heads of households, widows, pregnant women, mothers of young children or the elderly, as they have to carry all the daily responsibilities of survival on their shoulders, which consumes huge amounts of time and energy. Furthermore, camp authorities and aid organizations may not be aware of their situation, as in many cultures women are not in the public sphere and often do not even have their own identity documents, and because the specific needs of women are not taken into account in camps. For example, pregnant women required larger food rations and more access to health services. Also, women with children have a special concern for their children's education and often have to find ways to pay for their children's clothes and books, so if the children are in school, they have to face increased workloads.

On the other hand, women in displacement situations invariably lack the privacy necessary to maintain their personal hygiene and dignity. Having to share sleeping, cleaning and washing facilities with many people forces many women to choose between maintaining their personal hygiene and maintaining their dignity and safety.

Women are detained as a result of conflict, often in worse conditions than men. This is primarily because the majority of those detained are men, and there are very few prisons or places of detention exclusively for women. Consequently, in many cases women detainees are housed in male prisons and their smaller sections are generally the smallest and lack adequate sanitary and other facilities.

The existence of a separate prison for women can also give rise to problems. Since women usually constitute only a minority of detainees, very few prisons are built specifically for them. This means that the nearest women's prison may be located far from their home and being sent there separates them from their families and the support they can provide. Generally, detainees are very dependent on visits from relatives who bring them food and other extra items (such as medicines, clothes, toiletries, etc.). Women often suffer from the lack of family visits and thus the support of their families. There are many reasons for this: remoteness from the place where they are detained, insecurity for visitors, unwillingness or inability of relatives to come and visit (because they are displaced, have disappeared or cannot be contacted), or lack of money to pay the costs of the trip.

On the other hand, women in detention often have additional concerns about the welfare of their children, either because they have young children to raise in difficult conditions in the place of detention, or because they have been separated from their children and are affected by the uncertainty of not knowing who is raising them or how. Even when it is a family member who takes responsibility for the children, it can be very difficult for women to endure this enforced separation.

Women also have specific needs that are difficult to meet when they are in detention. For example, women and girls of menstruating age often have problems obtaining adequate health protection, regular access to sanitary facilities (toilets and washing areas) and appropriate clothing to experience their menstruation in a way that preserves their health and dignity. Often during detention, both men and women are subjected to abuse, including sexual violence. For women, there is a serious risk of pregnancy and gynaecological problems, in addition to the fear of the consequences this may have on their lives, both while in detention and after their release, when they return to their families and communities.

War causes extreme suffering to those who are caught up in it. Women experience war in many ways, from active participation as combatants to becoming targets of attack as members of the civilian population, specifically because they are women. But war for women does not only involve rape; it also involves separation, loss of family members and of the very means of subsistence, and brings with it injury and deprivation. War compels women to play unaccustomed roles and to develop new coping skills. Yet books and manuals treat them as passive players in the conflict.

Among the many pictorial manifestations that reveal the suffering, activism and situation of women in the war, the work of the German Käthe Kollwitz, born in Königsberg in 1867 and who was not only an artist but also a pacifist, stands out as a successful critic of the public. The violence of the wars in her context, as well as the loss of a son during the First World War, significantly marked the production of her works, and that has made her one of the most popular figures of German art among centuries today. The daughter of a Prussian social democrat and strongly influenced by the Lutheran religious ideas of her maternal grandfather, Käthe grew up in a hostile environment, suffering rejection in her village because of the ideas of her father and mother, who soon realized her talent and enrolled her in drawing and painting lessons before she was twelve years old, and moved to Berlin at the age of 16 to an art school for women. In 1887 she returned to her hometown, setting up her first studio and starting her painting production in a professional and independent way, at the same time that she made her first engraving.

In 1891 she married Dr. Karl Kollwitzr and they moved to Berlin, where they settled in one of the poorest districts of the capital. There her husband worked as both a doctor and an active socialist. Her husband's active militancy had a significant influence on Käthe Kollwitz's artistic works, since her view of the miserable living conditions of the working class and her political activism were central to her early works. In 1892 her son Hans was born, and in 1896 her son Peter.

In 1898 Käthe Kollwitz began teaching at the Berlin School for Women Artists, where she remained until 1903, and in 1910 she began her production of sculptures.

In 1914 her son Peter was killed in combat in Flanders, at the beginning of the First World War, a fact that conditioned all her artistic production, assuming one of the deepest reflections on the horror of violence and poverty in warlike conflicts felt by a woman. Rarely do female portraits acquire the dignity of beings who face the hardship and misery imposed as those made by Kollwitz and there are few occasions when we witness the courage and sincerity of a woman who observes herself, through her self-portraits, in an intimate act of sincerity and search for answers in a hostile, harsh and cruel world. The bodies of the women of Kollwitz acquire a character of truth and testimony, they get tired, they crawl and embrace strongly the life that snatches away misery and violence.

They rise up as a protective force in the face of the destruction of life. His two collections, "The Revolt of the Peasants" and "The Rise of the Weavers" symbolize how the poor classes confront power, women and men, and fight for a life of dignity. In them, women are an essential part of life, both sustaining it on a daily basis, preventing violence, and ultimately seeking the dead bodies of their children on the battlefield.

These are unusual images for a gaze accustomed to the beautiful and canonical bodies of Western art. They are the bodies of people impoverished by the economic crisis, by inequality, they are the image of unemployed people, taken to the corners of misery that they look at, that impel the look of the spectator, to ask. Rarely do we find the bodies of people, without idealization, with all of humanity, as in Käthe Kollwitz's work.

They are the image of those forced to go to the battlefield, to death, to disappearance. They recognize the injustice of a disembodied power that manipulates, condemns and orders, that prescribes and proscribes. But at the same time, Kollwitz shows us the greatest dignity in their bodies, their faces, their hands that embrace, assist and collect. The mother who embraces the son who died of misery in her arms, the group of women who close around them their children, the teenager who stands up against war, misery and injustice. The artist said, in her writings, that she found much more beauty in poverty than in the refined environments of the upper classes. In Kollwitz, ethics and aesthetics are united, where beauty is a moral category.

Despite the unpopularity of her opposition to the war, in 1919 she was appointed to the Prussian Academy of the Arts and became the first woman to hold a place in that institution, where she remained until her forced resignation in 1933, due to the rise to power of Hitler's National Socialist party, as happened to so many other members of her artistic generation.

Between 1920 and 1925 he produced the series Seven Woodcuts on War, published in 1924 along with the portfolio Parting and Death, and the following year he published the series The Proletariat, all of which were strong social critiques denouncing the most painful conditions of the war and the social injustices of the time. These woodcuts focused on the anguish suffered by wives, fathers and sons whose men fought and died in the war. In The Sacriface, a new mother offers her baby as a sacrifice to the cause. In The Widow II, a woman and her baby lie huddled together, perhaps starving.

These impressions express the raw agony that war inflicts on humanity. In The Widow I, a woman hugs herself in anguish. Her rounded shape and the tender touch of her massive hands on her chest and abdomen suggest that she may be pregnant, adding to the shock of her situation. In The Mothers, a group of women locked in a tight embrace comfort each other, while two frightened children peek out from under their protective group. In The Volunteers, four young people, whose grieving faces and clenched fists betray their sense of doom and determination, volunteer to fight as they follow a drummer figure in a death mask. Pain and torment permeate each of these images, graphically conveyed by the raw cuts in the woodcut medium. The Seven Woodcuts on the Kollwitz War is one of several portfolios of prints by German artists that focus on the savagery of World

War I. But instead of showing the brutalities of the war and the bombings experienced by the soldiers, the artist portrays the emotional responses of the civilians. Although her sense of loss was very personal because of the loss of her youngest son, Peter, Kollwitz represents universal visions of the endless sadness that war generates for those left behind.

Since the Nazis' rise to power, Kollwitz has been a victim of the harassment that characterized Hitler's regime against avant-garde artists. His works were included in the Exhibition of Degenerate Art held in Berlin, whose opening took place on July 19, 1937.

The period between 1937 and 1944 was especially tragic for Kollwitz. The continuous pressure of the Nazi regime was compounded by the destruction of his studio with almost all of his works during the Allied bombings. This vital pessimism can be seen in her last series of prints, Death (composed of eight lithographs), which seems to foresee the death of her husband in 1940 and her own death on

April 22, 1945, shortly before the end of the war, in Moritzburg, where she had moved two years earlier to the residence of a relative with the intention of going into hiding.

Kollwitz made a total of 275 woodcuts and lithographs. Virtually the only portraits she made during her lifetime were images of herself, of which there are at least fifty.

Today, perhaps her most emblematic work is an enlarged version of a similar sculpture by Kollwitz, Mother with her Dead Son, better known as The Kollwitz Pieta, which was placed in 1993 in the center of the Neue Wache in Berlin and serves as a memorial to the victims of war and tyranny.

The work of the German artist shows, without a doubt, the activism and victimhood of women in war, who, in addition to being hostile, civilians, victims of rape and violence, detained or imprisoned, do so as daughter, mother and wife.

THE TRAGIC END OF THE HONEYMOON: SANTIAGO RUSIÑOL'S "MORPHINE".

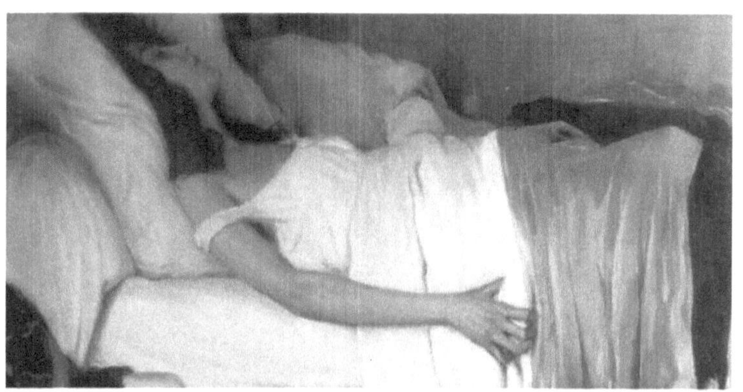

Santiago Rusiñol "The Morphine". 1894. Oil on canvas. 115 x 87,36 cm. Cau Ferrat Museum, Sitges, Barcelona.

As an incorruptible food, which becomes much sweeter as time passes, honey has become in many cultures a metaphor and symbol of eternal love, marital happiness and marriage. In the West, in the sixteenth century, newly married couples who wanted to have a boy had to drink mead for the entire lunar month following their wedding. From here we have inherited the current expression of "honeymoon".

However, 4000 years ago, already in the Babylonian culture, it was a custom that, for one month after the wedding, the father of the bride provided his son-in-law with all the honey beer he could drink. Since the Babylonian calendar was based on moon phases, this period was called the "honeymoon". In Ancient Rome the mother of the bride had to leave in the bedroom where the bride and groom were to sleep on their wedding night a pot of honey for the newlyweds. Honey was also considered a fertility enhancer. In some cases, it was extended to about a month. The Teutons, celebrated their weddings only under a full moon. After the celebration, the bride and groom had to drink a honey liqueur for 30 days to ensure a sweet life and a prolific family. Thus, today, the concept "honeymoon" refers to the trip that the newlyweds make full of expectations, projects and dreams that are probably far from the reality that ensues.

Interestingly, this same idyllic and mythical concept was used by the American psychologist Lenore E. Walker in her 1979 work "The Battered Woman", where she includes what the author calls "Cycle of abuse" or "Cycle of Violence" in reference to the cycle that victims of violence go through with respect to their abuser, and using it to identify one of the phases of a cycle that makes it impossible for abused women to think about and create alternatives to get out of the situation.

The author concluded that violence occurs in three phases that repeat themselves in a cyclical manner. These are:

The first is the phase of accumulation of tension. In this phase, tension increases within the couple, the man becomes increasingly angry with the woman for no apparent reason and verbal violence increases. These attacks are usually taken by the woman as isolated episodes that she can control and that will eventually disappear. Here there are small episodes that lead to permanent friction between the man and the woman, with a constant increase in anxiety and hostility. This phase can last for years, so if the victim seeks help, the acute phase or the shock can be prevented.

In the explosion or aggression phase, the situation explodes in the form of physical, psychological and/or sexual aggression. This is the stage where the woman, facing the blow, carries out the judicial denunciation. The physical violence becomes a detonator and that is why she tries to put an end to this crisis.

The cycle closes with a phase of calm, reconciliation or honeymoon in which the aggressor asks the woman for forgiveness, tells her that he is very sorry and that it will not happen again. He uses strategies of emotional manipulation to try to prevent the relationship from breaking up, such as giving her gifts, inviting her to dinner or a movie, making promises, showing affection, and reminding her of the man she fell in love with. The woman believes that the aggressor really wants to change, forgives him, withdraws the complaint if he has put it or not, without knowing that this reinforces his position.

In the above mentioned phases it can be seen that there is no physical violence, without a previous and parallel psychological violence. When the man asks her to forgive him, the woman trusts him again and leaves without effect the exposition made in the court. This is the moment when this situation becomes habitual and naturalised. This shows that violence is chronic, because it happens in a cyclical way. It is very important to detect the signs of help or signs that one as a friend or relative of a victim can detect. Separating oneself from one's intimate circle, stopping working, isolating oneself socially, becoming more shy, denying or justifying violence are some of the attitudes that will gradually become part of one's behaviour and personality.

After the "honeymoon" phase, violence becomes more consolidated, more frequent, escalates and its consequences are more serious.

Gender-based violence, largely exercised in the domestic sphere by men, is a complex and multifactorial problem based on mechanisms of domination of some people over others, of men subjugating women, pretending to point out who holds the power in the family framework with violent forms of interaction, as is the case of abusive relationships. Furthermore, these relationships are the result of a family and social model that has accepted them as valid strategies for the resolution of certain conflicts. This violence is a problem "for" women and a problem "of" men since it is mostly men who exercise violent behavior and women who suffer from it.

It is a tragedy framed in a social and cultural environment that has been tolerating and even encouraging these aggressions with the ideological consensus that justifies the internalization of victimizing roles by women, even anesthetizing their discomfort.

This "honeymoon" thus becomes a state of abnegation, dreaming, learned helplessness and, in too many cases, the ingestion of drugs that are intended to relieve pain and that immerse the victims in situations of greater risk.

At the beginning of the 19th century, opium was prescribed to "relieve" pain, without any certainty as to the recommended doses according to the purity of the preparation. Friedrich Serturner, a German chemist and pharmacist, became interested in the effects of opium very early on. At the age of 16, he was already an apprentice pharmacist and in 1809 had his first pharmacy. Four years earlier and while still an apprentice, Serturner decided, like many chemists of the time, to try to isolate the active ingredients of plants. He did a two-year job that led to the discovery of "morphine", a job that most colleagues rejected and did not consider valid, so he resorted to the only formula that would make his discovery an official finding and that was to carry out public experimentation on himself and three friends who volunteered. The idea was to prove that the substance he had isolated was in fact responsible for the actions of opium.

The work, which he had begun earlier, was based on his observations, which indicated that some samples had a clear pain-killing effect, while other samples did not. The chemist imagined that the opium must contain something that could counteract the pain, but that it could not work unless the dose was high enough. Using ammonia to separate the opium into its basic components isolated what he would later call morphine. Before testing his body, he began the first doses with mice and dogs he found in his neighborhood. They would all die on the way, but Serturner didn't give up. It was clear that he was right, so he went on to test his compound with three friends. The theory in this case was clear that this was the only way to test his study, and the four of them could clearly describe what was happening and what they were feeling.

So, at the age of 20, he distributed a first mixture of morphine and alcohol among the participants. The experiment and its effects lasted three days. By the end of the experiment, he and his three friends had consumed about 10 times what could now be recommended for a single dose of morphine. From his writings, he tells of a process where they experienced nausea, fever and dizziness. Serturner came to think that they were poisoned by the experiment, so they took vinegar in order to induce violent vomiting. They then went through a process described as a "long sleep". Finally, among the side effects of the morphine, he reported headaches, stomach aches and extreme fatigue that would last for several days.

Serturner succeeded in making the finding official, he had isolated the active ingredient of morphine. Not only that, the experimentation itself gave the opiate drug its name in honor of the Greek god of dreams, Morpheus, because of the profound effect of intense sleep. Thus, in 1817 Serturner marketed morphine as an analgesic, becoming the first treatment for opium and alcohol addiction.

The beginning of his experiment was historic because of the consequences that followed. Morphine became the first treatment of various symptoms in medicine. The mass use of it led to the appearance of hypodermic needles in 1843, which allowed for instantaneous and more powerful effects than their oral supply. With it came the first victim of overdose using the needles.

In 1878, an opiate was isolated by acetylation of morphine hydrochloride, resulting in diacetylmorphine. Most people will not understand the significance of this, but in 1898 diacetylmorphine was marketed by Bayer under the name of heroin. Yes, heroin was once "owned" by Bayer, and yes, it was also marketed as a cough sedative and/or as a substitute for morphine thinking it was less addictive. One of the great scourges of semi-synthetic drugs of consumption was therefore born, and derived from morphine itself (itself originating from the opium plant).

Morphine addict the Spanish painter, writer and playwright Santiago Rusiñol y Prats, in 1894 painted one of his best known works "La morfina", a work influenced by the impressionists, but intimate and symbolic. An oil on canvas measuring 115cm x 87.36 cm that is currently in the Cau Ferrat Museum in

Sitges, Barcelona, reveals the dramatic situation of a woman who could well be a victim of physical or psychological abuse and resorts to it to lull herself to sleep, forget, forgive and accept, only to return to the cycle of violence after eight to ten hours. The protagonist of the painting is a young woman whose hand still appears in tension, clinging strongly and dramatically to the sheet while her face reveals that the alkaloid has begun to take effect by transferring it to the worlds of Morpheus. The colour of the blanket, yellow, symbolises that she is sick.

The morphine in Spain, at the end of the 19th century was a drug widely spread and used by the society in general and by the high society especially. Women from the wealthier classes held meetings to inject themselves collectively, even ordering silver syringes from jewelers, in some cases even inlaid with diamonds. However, in spite of its diffusion, it was socially frowned upon, so Rusiñol resorted to the subterfuge of representing the young woman as a sick person, who would be taking the drug to alleviate her pain.

The difficulties of emotional expression, the weak self-esteem, the distorted perception of reality and the experience of constant threat, are the basis of many violent conflicts in the home. Therefore, the most frequent form of violence against women is domestic violence through repeated mistreatment by means of physical, sexual and/or psychological abuse. Pushing, beating, rape, insults, humiliation, threats or even murder are only some of the manifestations of these aggressions in the domestic sphere.

Some 24% of women between the ages of 18 and 64 are victims of abuse. Of these, 12% have ever considered suicide to end their situation. Even 6% of abused women have attempted to take their own lives at some point. Women who are physically or psychologically abused also suffer from psychopathological affliction, and a high number of them also suffer from forced sex. Despite this, it is estimated that 85% of domestic violence situations are not reported. However, the problem does not stop there, as despite the large number of complaints filed, most of them do not reach the pre-trial stage, because they are

208

withdrawn by the women in the face of pressure, feelings of guilt or fear of all kinds, or because they are poorly formulated in the difficult administrative procedures. Furthermore, the lack of legal or judicial support and the lack of knowledge of existing resources (shelters, supervised apartments, psychological counselling, etc.) do not help the complaints to follow their normal procedure.

With all these data, it can be considered that there is a certain lack of will to punish those who exercise violence in the family environment, which leads to multiple problems, both legal and, mainly, social.

It is inexplicable for society that women do not put an end to this situation, without understanding that they are in a spiral in which we must all get involved to rescue.

THE ESCALATION OF VIOLENCE AND CRIMES OF PASSION: FRAGONARD'S "THE LOCK".

Jean Honoré Fragonard "The Lock". 1776. Oil on canvas. 71 x 92 cm. Louvre Museum.

Wounding, burning, beating, pushing and finally killing are the last steps in a process of gender-based violence that begins in a slow, slow and continuous escalation years before the dramatic end, while the day-to-day is no less tragic.

Society must become aware that no one has the right to mistreat another person and there is no reason to do so. The only person responsible for the abuse is the one who practices it, not the victim. The mistreated woman must know that, no matter how much she expresses regret and tenderness, and no matter how much she tries, she will not change, and if she does not stop it as soon as possible, she will fall into an upward process where the intensity and frequency of the aggressions will increase as time goes by.

Love does not kill, nor does it hurt, nor does it distress, nor does it frustrate, nor does it frighten, however many women from the beginning of their relationships live it this way, confusing its possessiveness with a demonstration of love. "Nobody loves you like I do", "your friends are stupid, they look at me badly", "we have to spend more time together", "who is calling you", "who are you going with", "where are you going" are the first warning signs and the beginnings of psychological abuse, of controlling social relationships, of isolating her. The environment senses it, the family lives it, but they justify it because they think they are in love, when it comes to bad treatment.

The woman begins to distance herself from her friends, from her father, mother, brothers and sisters, and devotes her time to him, who generally confesses to her having had an unhappy and bitter childhood, making her believe that she is his redeemer, his savior and, without realizing it, becoming the punching bag where he pays for his frustrations and scorn, beginning the verbal violence. Insults, threats, coercion, contempt, first in private and later publicly that she continues to justify and defend believing that they are the ones to blame for these reactions.

Once this stage is normalized, sexual violence is promoted, forcing her to maintain contacts and relationships, when, where and how they want and preventing them from enjoying their sexuality freely. If not antecedent, in parallel, physical violence begins, forcing, pushing, hitting, slapping and, of course, later blaming her for provoking those reactions, humiliating her until she believes herself responsible and entering a phase of defenselessness that prevents her from denouncing.

It is not easy to denounce the person with whom you have made a life project, with whom you share a home or have sons or daughters in common. And it is not easy because they feel that if they do so, they break the family unit, and they are crushed by this issue. There is no profile of a victim, we can be any of us, violence does not depend on the economic level, nor on the formation, we can all be victims of abuse.

The insults, disdain, humiliation and blows can be prolonged for years, so when a woman is murdered it is not worth the phrase "there were no complaints", since this does not imply that there were no abuses, but rather fear and paralysis in interposing it. The murder, or attempted murder, of a woman by her partner or ex-partner is the tip of the iceberg of a prolonged relationship of abuse, never a one-time event or what was until recently called a "crime of passion".

Atrocities committed by men against women have been justified in the name of "passion", "love" and "romance". Killings or abuse within the home were left behind, in "domestic life". These were the times of unspoken things, of concealment and denial, of "couple problems. Still the media speak of crimes metaphorizing the triad of "love, madness and passion", when violence has to be treated as part of a process of explaining itself so that the subject ceases to be something "intimate and casual" and becomes social.

Cases of violence must leave the privacy of the home for public treatment. Headlines such as "she was found dead" or "the alleged murderer", when he has turned himself in and confessed, or invitations to neighbours who say "he was a nice, polite man" are inadmissible.

In that same atmosphere of eroticism, debauchery and "love affairs", the history of art speaks of masterpieces, intimist and genre. Representations such as the well-known "The Bolt", "Le Verrou" or "The Bolt" by the French painter Jean-Honoré

Fragonard , an oil on canvas made between 1776 and 1779 whose dimensions are 71 cm x 92 cm and which we can see in the Louvre Museum in Paris, invites us to go deeper into the subject.

The patriarchal culture and the androcentric historiography have catalogued this work as a gallant scene that shows two lovers intertwined in a bedroom, a masterpiece of the French rococo and the artist as one of the best representatives of scenes of love and pleasure, of voluptuousness and mastery of luminosity. Indeed, in this work we can see that the mastery of light and colour accentuates the drama of the event, which was once seen as a passionate scene, but with a gender perspective we cannot ignore that it is a situation of abuse, an episode in the escalation of physical violence that has overcome psychological and verbal violence and anticipates sexual violence.

In the canvas there are two main protagonists, the man and the woman; and two secondary ones, the lock and the bed, all of them forming a closed, internal space of penumbra in the adversity.

The young, libertine man, with light, loose, unbuttoned, white and silk clothes, barefoot, with his hair loose and disordered, energetically grabs the lady, young, beautiful, noble or bourgeois, dressed in satin, who resists with her hand removing her face, and with her body and her strength rejecting him. Before her anguish, and stretching out his right arm, the man without letting go of her closes the door by armoring a lock, functionally badly placed but, which serves to exaggerate his intention and transmit her tension and defenselessness. The bed, on the right and undone, incites to think that the struggle has begun before the snapshot of the captured scene, a scene of rape without a doubt, understood in its moment as erotic or of passion. When, without a doubt, the name of the work locks the lady in the room, isolating her and preventing her from enjoying her freedom.

When we hear that there has been a murder of a woman at the hands of her partner or ex-partner, let us not forget, however much they hide it, that there has been a prelude to psychological, verbal, sexual and physical abuse. When the blows come, the victim is already isolated, when the murder, is that physically or emotionally has been beaten.

It's not no. There's no more.

THE VULNERABILITY OF THE PREGNANT WOMAN AND THE WORK OF GUSTAV KLIMT.

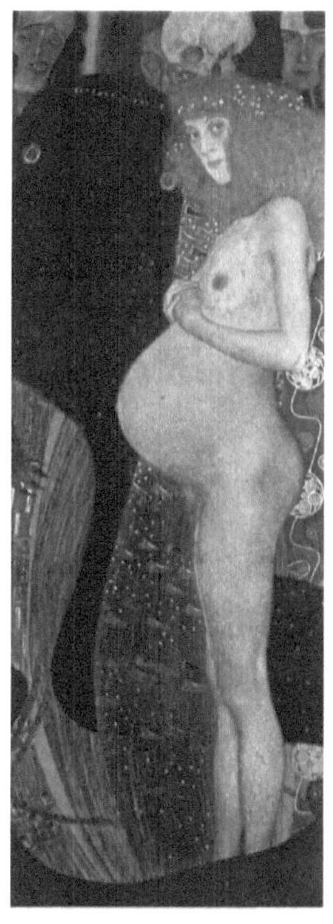

Gustav Klimt "Hope I". 1903. Oil on canvas. 189 x 67 cm. National Gallery of Canada.

Gestation and motherhood are possibly the two moments that change a woman's life, producing physical, psychological and emotional changes that make them a vulnerable population at maximum risk. Statistics tell us that almost one in four women (22.7%) suffers verbal, physical or sexual gender-based violence during pregnancy.

In 1903, the Austrian symbolist painter Gustav Klimt, painted "Hope I", whose protagonist is a pregnant woman. In his painting "Medicine" he had already dealt with the subject, but in a more subtle, less evident way. Of course, the work was a scandal in his time, a puritanical Austrian society, so although the artist made it to exhibit that year in the building of the Secession, the Minister of Culture Von Hartel, convinced Klimt not to do it and prevent the controversy from increasing in the universities. The painter accepted and soon found a buyer in the co-founder of the Vienna Workshops, Fritz Wärndonfer, who kept it covered with a canvas for years. Today the canvas is on display at the

National Gallery of Canada and measures 189 x 67 cm.

The work is a clear example of the artist's symbolist style, although he does not use the peculiar gold leaf in his production, the sinuous forms and the decorative elements become indicative of his personal style. The lack of perspective and the horror vacui are also characteristic of this work, one of his masterpieces in which we can see the high quality of the drawing and its ease in applying colour.

Titled "Hope I" and translated as "Esperanza I", it is an oil on canvas whose protagonist is a pregnant woman, totally naked, standing and holding her hands together on her stomach and close to her breast. The model for the work was Herma, a woman who had already posed for Klimt on several occasions but who stopped going to his studio because of her pregnancy. When the painter found out about this, he called her to pose, since her economic needs were combined with the possibility of dealing with a new, unusual and provocative subject for the society of the time, with which she was once again entering into controversy. Klimt represented Herma as young, very young, infantilized, if it were not for her bulging belly no one would think she was pregnant. Her adolescent legs, her youthful breasts, her fragile arms, her childish face and her thick red hair, equal to the color of her pubic hair, are crowned by white flowers that are an allegory of her innocence. The model's age and physiognomy are unknown at the time but, consciously or unconsciously, the truth is that the pregnant woman is far from the physical patterns of a woman in her eighth or ninth month of gestation, but they are right in the collective imaginary created around a woman in that state and that, socially, as soon as she knows that she is on tape the patriarchal culture returns her to childhood, no longer treating her as a woman and, regardless of her age, turning her into a child lacking in autonomy, criteria and abilities.

Regardless of whether she is an adult or an adolescent, whether she is alone or in a couple, whether she is autonomous, intelligent or capable, whether she has a precarious job or not, when a woman announces her motherhood, her self-confidence is automatically undermined both in the family and in the health field, and she is tried to become a docile being who abides by the criteria of others, becoming a "primip". Her physical constitution, her weight, the food that she eats, her habits and even her movements are judged, so that what should be a moment of happiness, personal harmony and transition, is generated in her the belief that she is in a dangerous and risky situation that both have to control, losing her freedom and sovereignty. She begins to talk to them using diminutives, with a condescending language, relegating the role of the protagonist to one of mere spectators of the actions they exercise on their reified bodies. Paternalism hovers over her without respecting her autonomy or decision-making capacity, treating her as a patient or a sick person instead of an adult or a user.

In the family environment, mothers-in-law, mothers, sisters, sisters-in-law become reminders and prescriptions based on their experiences, even neighbors or strangers dare to give advice that is not asked for but that is loaded with reason. Situations are developed where, instinctively, women begin to compete obsessively transmitting stress, worry and fears to the future mother in circumstances that should be of absolute relaxation.

At the health level, although the issue of obstetric violence must be addressed more broadly, when faced with a pregnant woman, the professional in a white coat treats her as a child, imposing treatment and performing interventions without asking for her consent. The number of ultrasound scans above the necessary, excessive vaginal touches, episeotomies, stimulation with synthetic oxytocin to plan schedules and hospital staff, use of forceps, amniotomies, unnecessary cesarean sections, are some revealing examples of how health care kidnaps the autonomy and capacity of women and decides, without taking into account their opinion, their body or sexuality, since, without informing us, these interventions will influence our future quality of life. In both areas we women feel pressured and coerced so that others decide for us, manipulate us, turn us into objects and annul our decision making.

Returning to Klimt's work, and once the infantilization of the protagonist has been interpreted, looking behind the clarity of her figure we see behind and to the right some disturbing and threatening figures that the pregnant woman seems to ignore. At the base and trapping her feet is a sea monster whose tail is wrapped around her trying to capture her and going out of frame. To her left, behind her, black, there seems to be Typhoon, another ox-headed monster born from the union of Gaya (mother earth) and Tartarus (the deepest and most inhospitable place in the underworld) and who depending on the moment could moo like a bull, roar like a lion, bark like a pack of hounds or speak the language of the gods. With his different noises he intended to dominate the world. In the painting he appears with a crown of stars on his sloping forehead that lights his way. In the background there are four figures, the most evident being a skull that extends to her feet in a bluish mantle decorated with golden stars, and which symbolizes death; the other three faces are malignant connotations that could elude illness, madness and panic. The work is thus contrasted with the sweet image of her with the evils and fears of which the young woman does not seem to be aware.

The advances in medicine since Klimt painted his work until today have improved the levels of birth and reduced the risks in pregnancy and childbirth, but without a doubt and emotionally the women on tape continue to worry about the health of their future babies, their fears and apprehensions, despite the advances, persist. The monsters of the modernist painter's work lead us to reflect on the one that unfortunately emerges in too many cases alongside the pregnant woman, and that is the violent abuser, and that is that today we have indicators that indicate that the predominance of physical and sexual abuse is greater and more serious among pregnant women than among other women, making them a severe risk group.

With the pregnancy, the jealousy of the male who stops receiving the same care is unleashed, many even doubt or suspect that they are responsible. Their possessiveness leads some to prevent them from going to the doctor, touching them or seeing them because they consider their bodies their own. Many see the event as an economic burden both because of the expenses of the future baby and because of the woman's physical indisposition to continue with the same work inside and outside the home. There are also those who take advantage of their vulnerability and helplessness to pay for their anger and frustration with their bodies, as well as to develop a paternalistic and dominant macho role.

The sweet wait or the state of good hope becomes for many a humiliating, shameful, silent and lonely ordeal in which they begin to discover the monster who has impregnated them and, unfortunately, with whom they will have a lifelong bond. If it is repugnant for a man to attack a woman, it is even more repugnant for him to do so while she is pregnant, and even more repugnant for him to attempt against the life of a defenseless being who has not been born and of whom he is biologically the progenitor.

Weight gain, discomfort, physical changes due to fluid retention and increased volume of the belly, stretch marks on the chest and other parts of the body, hormonal changes that cause nausea, breast pain, acne outbreaks, constipation and emotional disturbances are the minimal changes we suffer in pregnancy. Our lives change, we seek recollection, we need peace, healthy food, have adequate schedules, rest, go from caring for them and please them to take care of ourselves and the baby we are carrying. In this metamorphosis, abandonment of the canon of beauty and dethronement of the prince, many men, in a rude, cruel and ruthless way, decide to continue with their lives without assuming their paternity.

A good friend called Leticia told me one day that, before she knew she was pregnant, she went out every weekend with her partner, drinking and having fun until she couldn't. With the pregnancy she stopped going out at night; he kept doing it. He came back in the morning, loaded, reeking of alcohol, wanting to have sex. In her second month of pregnancy she received her first slap which was the prelude to beatings, humiliation and humiliation until a premature birth. Another friend, Rosario, due to complications in her pregnancy, had to abandon the precarious job she had cleaning houses in order to depend economically on him. Ugly, whore, crazy, were the insults she received when she asked for something. Almudena, another friend, spent her pregnancy crying, suffering rape, wanting to leave and enduring being told how useless she was and where a misfortune like her with a daughter or pregnant woman could go. My three friends gave birth to their babies in loneliness and bitterness, far from the dream that they had idealized, and when they saw that the abuse persisted on them and their children, they abandoned them. My three friends endured a contentious process that ended in a shared custody exercised by the parents to continue mistreating them.

The myth of motherhood ceases to be so when we enter into these cases, which one out of every four women who live with a partner endures, then we have the case of single adult women who rarely have family support when they decide to become pregnant, as well as that of teenagers who, without yet having, as is normal, the capacity for judgment and judgement, leave childhood to enter adulthood by force.

Those cries without apparent reasons that literature speaks of may correspond in reality to the discovery of the prince that came out of you frog, with the feeling of having made a mistake impossible to repair, with discovering that it is late to take solutions and accept that you have to endure.

Slaps, pushes, punches, kicks, wounds, beatings, burns, broken bones, hair pulling, throwing objects, hair cuts, insults, humiliations, rapes, beatings in the belly to make her have an abortion, hospital admissions, infections, bleeding, it is the daily life of many pregnant women.

If violence against a woman is a criminal act in itself, doing so against the pregnant woman, besides being abominable, triggers the risks and prolongs them for the fetus.

The reproductive capacity of women should be a reason for their empowerment but unfortunately patriarchy has used it to subject us and make us vulnerable. This is another struggle that needs to be addressed.

Conclusion

Feminist training is necessary because it is the only way to guarantee equal education. Making history and the past visible, studied and analysed is the best way to understand the inequalities that have existed on the basis of gender.

Artistic productions, as reproductions of past mentalities, are a fundamental vehicle for humanistic education, as well as an inexhaustible source for social debate.

Art and its history must cease to be conceived as passive elements of knowledge that are exhibited in silent museums and become socializing agents through active dialogue.

Women have been and are an object in the service of patriarchy. We can see this through works of art history.

Reified images, created from ideals of beauty at the whim of the male, artists made invisible, female artistic productions undervalued, scenes admired in museums and institutions that contain abductions, abuse, aggression or rape.

Turbulent lives under the cover of being educated in the belief of romantic love, standard-bearers of feminism, fears, dreads, dates to remember.

Myths, legends and stories that cover up aberrations, stereotypes and archetypes that have survived until today.

This book reflects on all of this through works of art.

The study of art and its relationship with women has just begun. There are many biographies that must be redone with other parameters and much gender perspective to apply to art. This is therefore a new and risky version that should not leave anyone indifferent, for better or worse.

We are used to relating gender violence with murder, ignoring that which is exercised from other spheres such as the family, sexual, economic, intellectual, physical, historical, academic, institutional, cultural, religious or political.

It is this author's desire to put all these issues on the table by creating debate and criticism and, by bringing works of art closer to society as a tool in training in equality. Education is the only way to put an end to male violence.

I hope that, at the end of this book, we will feel the art closer to us and we will guess in the works that will be put before our eyes to men and women, first of all to people, victims of a patriarchal society.

Bibliography

Alexandrian, S. (1980 [1977]). Los libertadores del amor. Trad. Adolfo Sarabia Santander. Badalona: Ruedo ibérico.

Addis, S. (1989). The Art of Zen: Paintings and Calligraphy by Japanese Monks 1600-1925. Nueva York: Harry N. Abrams.

Ballester Buigues, I. (2012). El cuerpo abierto, Representaciones extremas de la mujer en el arte contemporáneo. Gijón: Trea.

Breton, A. (1972 [1924]) Los pasos perdidos. Madrid: Alianza editorial. Trad. Miguel Veyrat.

Caballero Guiral, J. (2002). La mujer en el imaginario surreal. Figuras femeninas en el universo de André Breton. Castellón: Universitat Jaume I.

Chadwick, W. (1992 [1990]). Mujer, arte y sociedad. Trad. María Barberán. Barcelona: Destino.

De Cecco, E. y Romano, G. (2002). Contemporanee. Percorse e poetiche delle artiste degli anni ottanta a oggi. Milano: Postmedia.

Lebovici, E. (2009). La gêne du féminin. En Elles @centrepompidou. París: Centre Pompidou.

Leymann, H. (1996). The Content and Development of Mobbing at Work. European Journal of Work & Organizational Psychology. Vol. 5. Issue 2, 165-184.

Marín Torres, J. M. (2008). Silencio y filosofía (Pensar en, desde, contra el silencio). En M. Farrell y M. Dos (Eds.), Veintinueve maneras de concebir el silencio. Castellón: Diputación provincial.

Marinetti, F. T. (1983, [1919]). Contro il matrimonio. En Democrazia futurista. Dinamismo politico, en Teoria e invenzione futurista, a cura di Luciano di Maria. Milano: Mondadori.

Nicoïdski, C. (1994). Une histoire des femmes peintres. Francia: Jean-Claude Lattès.

Nochlin, L. (1994 [1971]). Why Have There Been No Great Women Artists? En L. Nochlin, Women, Art, and Power and Other Essays (pp. 145-178). London: Thames & Hudson.

Pizan, C. (de) (1995 [1405]). La ciudad de las damas. Traducción de Maire-José Lemarchand. Madrid: Siruela.

Pollock, G. (1994). Histoire et politique: l'histoire de l'art peut-elle survivre au féminisme? En Féminisme, art et historie de l'art. París: École Nationale Supérieure des Beaux-Arts.

Weininger, O. (1985 [1902]). Sexo y carácter. Traducción del alemán de Felipe Jiménez de Asúa. Barcelona: Península.

Weidner, M. (Ed.). (1990). Flowering in the shadows. Women in the History of Chinese and Japanese Painting. Honolulu, Hawai: University of Hawaï Press.

www.ingramcontent.com/pod-product-compliance
Lightning Source LLC
Chambersburg PA
CBHW031058250726
48655CB00004B/1499